PEARLS OF WISDOM:

A Second Strand

Compiled by
Patricia Crane, Ph.D.
and
Rick Nichols

The
Crane's Nest

Cover & Book Design
by Rick Nichols

The information in this book is designed to impart information to help individuals in making positive changes in their lives. The ideas presented are not meant to substitute for medical care or psychological assistance.

Published by:
The Crane's Nest, a division of Health Horizons.
P.O. Box 1081
Bonsall, California, 92003
(800) 969–4584
www.heartinspired.com

ISBN: 1-893705-20-X
Self Help/Inspirational

DEDICATION

On behalf of the authors in this anthology we lovingly dedicate it to all travelers on the pathways of life. May every breathtaking summit, tooth jarring pothole, serene meadow, and dark and lonely wood, reward you with radiant pearls of wisdom, which you too may someday use to light the way for fellow travelers.

Namasté

CONTENTS

INTRODUCTION

*"In the middle of the road of my life
I awoke in a dark wood
where the true way was wholly lost."*
-Dante

Above are the opening lines to Dante's epic poem on existence, the *Commedia*. At some point in our lives, each of us will be in the place Dante describes, where we seem to be standing alone with nothing but our faith and inner strength to see us through. Oh, what a frightening yet magical place this can be, a place where we can learn about ourselves and the amazing powers we all possess to see us through the darkest night.

Most of the authors in this anthology are writing about their personal experience of that place and what they learned from it. You will read stories about healings of body, mind, spirit, relationship, and financial challenge. Some of these healings came painfully, others in a pleasant sort of way, and still others on a wave of laughter. As you will soon discover on the following pages—whatever way we become awakened in our own "dark wood", the operative word is *awakened*, and that is ultimately good.

So what is it that moves our storytellers to expose their wounds and their scars? Why would they reveal in intimate detail, their fears, their pain, their failures, and their losses? Most of them are not professional writers, and for some, writing in English is quite challenging as it is not their native language. There are, of course, a variety of motivations. But for most we think the strongest motivation is bridge building, as in the poem below. Through sharing their stories they are in effect, building bridges to help others span the tide.

An old man, going a lone highway,
came at the evening, cold and gray,
to a chasm, vast and deep and wide,
through which was flowing a sullen tide.
The old man crossed in the twilight dim;
the sullen stream had no fears for him;
but he turned when safe on the other side
and built a bridge to span the tide.

"Old man," said a fellow pilgrim near,
"You are wasting strength with building here;
your journey will end with the ending day;
you never again must pass this way;
you have crossed the chasm, deep and wide
why build you the bridge at the eventide?"

The builder lifted his old gray head;
"Good friend, in the path I have come," he said,
"There followeth after me today
a youth whose feet must pass this way.
this chasm that has been naught to me
to that fair-haired youth may a pitfall be.
He, too, must cross in the twilight dim;
good friend, I am building the bridge for him."

The Bridge Builder
by Will Allen Dromgoole

It is our sincere hope that you will find at least some of these "bridges" helpful as you make your own way along the astonishing pathways of life. And if you do at some point find yourself "wholly lost in a dark wood" perhaps the following words will help you find your way. They are words of wisdom from a Native American elder that would be offered to someone who asks the question, "What do I do if I am lost in a dark forest?" This version is rendered in the form of a poem by David Wagoner, and it is called, *Lost.*

> Stand still. The trees ahead and bushes
> beside you
> Are not lost. Wherever you are is called Here,
> And you must treat it as a powerful stranger,
> Must ask permission to know it and be known.
> The forest breathes. Listen. It answers.
> I have made this place around you.
> If you leave it, you may come back again,
> saying Here.
> No two trees are the same to Raven.
> No two branches the same to Wren.
> If what a tree or a bush does is lost on you,
> You are surely lost. Stand still. The forest
> knows
> Where you are. You must let it find you.

One way of reading this native wisdom is to know that wherever we are is Here. Here, the place where we are standing in this now, and that if we are willing to become aware of that place, come to know it as intimately as possible, and honor it ("let It find us"), than It will show us the way.

You see, we're never really lost, we just sometimes don't know how to get to where we think we want to go from where we are in the moment. "Stand still. The forest knows where you are. You must let it find you."

Love and blessings,

Patricia & Rick

June 5, 2006
San Diego, California

NOTE: Our authors are from many cultures around the world, and they speak to us in diverse ways. Throughout the editing process we have taken pains to retain as much of this diversity as possible. Therefore, you will discover words spelled in ways that are unfamiliar to you, and some sentence structures that may seem a bit odd to the North American English reading eye. To help you digest all of this, you will find the author's name and the name of their homeland just below the title at the beginning of each story.

IN GIVING WE RECEIVE

Sandra J Filer, Texas

*"Grandma time was very special time. A time of
leaving the ordinary to step into the enchanting."*

My grandmother and I shared a magical relationship. Grandma allowed me to dream. Never having a daughter yet always wanting one endeared me to her. As I was growing up, my Grandparents would frequently baby-sit. Once Grandpa departed for the day, all the dazzle came out. The bedroom closets were filled with baubles, beads, shoes, fur coats, and hats. A seemingly endless bounty of treasures awaited me during my magical visits. Something I remember very well is the time I spent on the floor reveling with her earring tree. For hours, I was allowed to play with Grandma's earrings, mink coats, and sparkly slippers. I can fondly remember Grandma smiling and laughing as I would twirl around in all of my magnificence. During this time of total elation, I was also completely enraptured by the vision of my glamorous self in her full-length mirror. "Grandma time" was very special time. A time of leaving the ordinary to step into the enchanting. Our relationship flourished.

As an adult, I would travel several times a year to stay with Grandma in Florida. Rather than play with an earring tree, I was now allowed carte blanche to wear whatever jewels were available in her endless chest of drawers. We also greatly enjoyed getting all dressed up to dine out together. In preparation, I would fix her hair as well as touch up her makeup. The annual trips to Florida were escapes for me. They became a time for connection. A time to play. A time to laugh. A time to experience the unconditional love of a Grandmother.

As she began to age, our adventures lessened. Our visits became a bit lower key. At the end of each visit, I would quietly walk out to the end of her beautifully painted driveway, late at night, under the big moon and all the stars to pray that the trip would not be my last. One day, it was. After a fall, Grandma's mobility decreased significantly. Being so far away logistically made it difficult to ensure that she was safe. The time came when a very difficult family decision was made to move Grandma into an assisted living center in Michigan. This was a trying time for everyone. My fun, magical Grandma was aging rapidly. And, worst of all, she was not happy!

Arriving at the retirement center, seeing her room for the very first time, was sobering to say the least. On the surface, we all celebrated how wonderful her small space was. How perfect it was for her. (I believe we were all doing this more for ourselves than for her.) There was a growing sadness inside of me. All I could visualize was her change from waking up in "paradise" (as she described it) to wearing diapers and eating when being instructed to do so. Touring the facility, we all saw, in my judgment, some lonely elders. It was then that I vowed to return to Texas and volunteer at retirement centers. If my Grandma was in Michigan with Grandchildren unable to visit, then there were Grandparents in Texas that needed adoptive Grandchildren too! So, that is what I did.

I began volunteering by offering facials to the residents. This led to calling bingo, attending field trips, Halloween story telling, Wal-Mart runs, etc. I fell in love with the elder residents and visited often. During bingo one day, I met a woman that reminded me of my Grandmother. The resemblance was uncanny. Mrs. Stewart not only looked like my Grandmother she was also a serious card player. They both stashed Saltine crackers in their wheelchair bags. They each kept score of things in a tiny little notebook. And, Mrs. Stewart seemed to have the exact same expressions on her face using her hazel eyes as my Grandma! Naturally, I was completely drawn to her. We became fast friends.

One day, on my way out the door to conduct facials, I received a phone call from my Father. It was April 30. This would be a day I would never forget. I was told that my Grandmother had fallen down. After further evaluation, she was diagnosed with lung cancer. With my heart breaking, I poured more love into the residents. One day, preparing for the King and Queen Ball, my favorite resident was on the Court. Mrs. Stewart was a contender for resident Queen. I had the privilege of preparing her skin and doing her royal makeup for the competition.

Once finished, she looked into the mirror with huge tears in her eyes. She said, "Oh my, is that me? I look beautiful." I said, "Mrs. Stewart, you are beautiful." As I was cleaning the table and putting away my items, I saw her wheelchair go by. Then I looked again to discover her backing up. Dead center in the doorway, she was watching me. I said, "Mrs. Stewart is there something I can do to help you?" Her response changed my life forever. For it was in this moment that I realized how the seemingly smallest acts of kindness can bring love and light into this world. Mrs. Stewart looked at me and said, "I just wanted to tell you that this was the best day of my life."

As I walked out to the car, I wept. I also filled up with love. This experience fueled my desire to share with others what a difference we can make by connecting. My Grandmother and Mrs. Stewart left this Earth within 90 days of each other afflicted by the same disease. I am so grateful that the love my Grandmother showered me with as a magical little girl resulted in my passing on that love to Mrs. Stewart and others.

I love you both - Grandma and Mrs. Stewart. May you both be winning at bingo in Heaven.

THE GIFT WORTH WAITING FOR

Victoria DePaul, Massachusetts

*"Conflicts in families and relationships
will end when all persons involved can
give up their need to be right."*

I think of Ms. Joyce as my second Mom, a spiritual Mom of sorts. We share a special bond of friendship and camaraderie and yet it is so much more than that. Ms. Joyce is a brilliant woman. In her 83 years of life she has maintained a keen interest in literature, history, the arts, philosophy and current events; we never lack topics for conversation.

I met Ms. Joyce through my friendship with her daughter Veronica. The family was assembling because of the sudden, unexpected death of Veronica's daughter. The first time we met I felt as though I was entertaining royalty (and of course now I know I was—a true regal spirit). Ms. Joyce and other members of the family arrived at Veronica's home earlier than anticipated. Veronica was not available so I stepped up to the plate and assumed my role as friend, neighbor and hostess.

As the family hails from the United Kingdom I made an immediate offer of tea which was graciously accepted.

I scurried for mugs and teabags and placed them in the microwave. As I turned around with the awkwardness that accompanies all encounters with new persons, particularly one where grief is present, I was met with horrified stares. Ms. Joyce, eyes wide said, "Surely you will not be serving tea from mugs in a microwave. Where is the teapot? Veronica must have a teapot!" A teapot, those were really for tea? In my house, and I suspect many other American households, teapots were for decorating shelves, storing pennies, dust collectors.

The four of us, me, Ms. Joyce and two of her daughters searched cabinets and shelves and eventually uncovered a teapot. I stared at the pot wondering how I was supposed to make tea with this. Being creative and wanting to please I filled it with water, placed 20 teabags inside with the tags ever so neatly lined on the edges, replaced the cover as best as I could and placed the pot in the microwave. The looks of horror had not diminished but by now we had all come to the silent conclusion that if we were going to get anywhere near a cup of tea on this day, resignation was the best option.

As the tea continued to brew in the microwave, Ms. Joyce asked, "Do you know where Veronica keeps the cozy?" A cozy...no chance I could fake this one. She returned to the cupboard where the teapot was found and pulled out a cozy and handed it to me. It was the strangest pot holder I had ever seen and quite awkward to use, my hand just didn't fit, but I appreciated that she was concerned that I might burn myself when I removed the teapot from the microwave. She watched, obviously amused, as I clumsily poured the tea into mugs. As she accepted the tea she said with a smile, "Tea from bags in a teapot in a microwave, how interesting." Does tea come from someplace other than a teabag? I made a mental note to investigate that at some future point.

Such was our introduction. Over the next months and years our paths crossed many times. In the past three years the family has had five deaths and two sisters with cancer. Throughout these trying times Ms. Joyce and I became quite close. Veronica and another daughter, Karen were both diagnosed with cancer at the same time. Ms. Joyce struggled in her advanced years to care for them both. I provided as much assistance as I could to lighten the load. It was during these months that our relationship blossomed. She called me her fifth daughter, a position I cherished.

We spent hours discussing current world events and politics. Ms. Joyce lived in London during WWII and offered a personal perspective of history that I could never have obtained from a text. We also debated for many an hour God, religion and spirituality. She was never quite sure what she believed and described herself as somewhere between atheism and agnosticism. I, on the other hand, have no such doubts. I shared with her my absolute certainty in God and a benevolent universe. While somewhat skeptical she allowed me my new age beliefs and many a lively conversation ensued.

One day she was particularly despondent. When I asked what was wrong, she asked me, "Do you believe in world peace?"

I replied without hesitation, "Absolutely, why do you ask?"

"My children just don't get along. I am an old woman and I'm so tired of it. They're grown now. Why can't they just get along?" I let her go on. "I'm so tired of the fighting. All they do is fight. I turn on the news and there's more fighting. It will never end. I know you have this belief in God and spirit and all that stuff but I don't see it."

I don't know if she wanted an answer but I gave her one anyway. I explained to her that people don't

7

get along because they don't allow others to truly be themselves. We all carry around a mental check-list of how others should be, act and think. When we observe that others do not meet our expectations of acceptable thought and behavior then conflict becomes inevitable because people seek to move others to conformity. Conflicts in families and relationships will end when all persons involved can give up their need to be right.

This goes further than simple tolerance. For true peace to be had not only must we be willing to forego our check-list for others we must also foster an environment where the other has total freedom to be as they are, each holding to the tenet of their own check-list for self and no other. That is Love; allowing the other total freedom and space to be as they are, as they choose to be. Love offers acceptance and fully embracing the other without requirement. Most relationship conflicts would disappear with this one practice: space must be given to the other to be as they are. When we can get to this point, not only will we enjoy peace in our families and neighborhoods, world peace can truly be had.

I offer my own life as testimony to the ability to live without conflict. I have no requirements, hold no grudges and therefore live a life rich in humor, joy and serenity.

And so we debated, Ms. Joyce and I. When all was said she agreed I had a good theory but couldn't see that it could ever really happen, people being who they are. As we continued to dialogue on this topic for weeks and months, she came to the conclusion that maybe the best she could do was to let the situation be as it is, to give up her requirement that they be able to get along. And so she found her peace, not from the requirement that her children be in harmony, but by allowing the situation to be as it is.

Today, as I've learned Ms. Joyce is dying, I reflect on our many conversations. Although she often disagreed with my spiritual philosophy she always allowed me space and love to be me. She gave me total freedom to be Who I Am, without requirement. That is love, the only love that is real, and the most precious gift we can receive.

MOVING BEYOND SUCCESS

Katrin Muff, Switzerland

*"As an adolescent, my father had told me
that the reason why people get down was
because reality didn't match their fantasy."*

Walking into Pushkin Square with confident steps, my lungs filled with frozen air and time slowed down. I had just come from acquiring a major contract that confirmed our business had overcome the uncertainty of its fragile evolution, assuring profitability. As I relaxed, an immense weight fell off my shoulders and I noticed snowflakes dancing in the air.

For a long time, I had aspired to become a leader, to make a difference. This dream had become a driving force in proving that I could successfully run a business. I had joined a leading global company and due to sweat, luck and stamina, at age 26 I was their youngest-ever general manager, in charge of a start-up window manufacturing business in Russia. During the two years in Moscow, with no single day going according to plan, I was stretched to new realms of courage, faith and determination. Success, to me, was a yardstick to measure how well I would realize my dream.

Tuning into a Soviet love song that played from the loudspeakers, my heart soared. The crunch of crisp snow under my shoes triggered an overwhelming realization: I had made it. Never had I felt so accomplished in my life. Silence settled within me: everything was finally perfect.

The following winter, I moved to the Netherlands. I had requested a sabbatical to digest the intense experience of running a business in Russia and to consider what to do next. The transition was tough: no phone rang, no emergencies, nobody who needed my direction, advice or support. I felt useless. Why was I feeling so hollow after having realized my dream?

As my professional mask dissolved, I gained access to a more intuitive, playful side of myself. Sharing an apartment with my childhood friend, "dressing down" to what young women my age wore, and taking theatre and creative writing classes, I finally tasted the lightheartedness of being in my twenties.

As I contemplated my future, I started redefining success. How could I avoid the trap of the stifling void that seemed to follow realizing a dream? Reviewing my Moscow experience in search of answers, I discovered that having been able to help others find their potential touched me much deeper than having proven myself. In this spirit, I co-founded a Dutch-Swiss venture and moved back to Switzerland. Our ambition was to help young companies and start-up teams off the ground with financing and coaching.

Life-work balance became important and I engaged with numerous experts to pursue my personal development. All went smoothly until two realizations coincided: one professional, the other personal. The market started turning against us and I discovered that I had been measuring myself against external standards rather than defining my own principles. We decided to liquidate the business and I chose to take some time off.

The void that grew out of burying our dream was profound, yet not as frightening as after Moscow. This time, I felt drawn to explore this silent space that seemed capable of triggering the best and worst of sensations. I thus started to explore new dimensions that were opening up to me. Learning to navigate in this new territory, I got lost frequently and flirted a few times with the option of turning back to the world that operated by rules I had already mastered. Yet, little by little, that quiet place inside became familiar, comfortable and increasingly influential.

While my strategic mind was busy figuring out my professional direction, I responded to people who approached me for support in a variety of challenging situations, both professional and personal. These people sought the human being in me, not the person fulfilling a professional role. They inspired me to let go of my professional shields of protection, freeing me to become what they were seeking: a pure presence of potential. Surprisingly, my coaching and training activities developed without a clear plan, but as a result of responding.

As an adolescent, my father had told me that the reason why people get down was because reality didn't match their fantasy. It had taken a long time to find out that accepting reality didn't kill my ability to shape my future. Instead, it enabled me to gain access to resources previously unavailable. Success started to become something to *be* rather than something to *have;* here and now, rather than in the future.

The first time I consciously experienced the power of effortless creation was in the summer of 2005 when I let go of my largest corporate coaching contract. When our collaboration approached a turning point, rather than elaborating on ways to continue, I remained silent. We eventually decided to let our achievements rest as they were. While this made my head spin in view of the financial consequences, my heart jumped at the chance to align with new opportunities.

In the weeks that followed, creativity surged. A dream kept appearing: integrating coaching with golf. I had been playing golf for a few years and respected the game for its blunt capacity to uncover personal limitations. To me, it had become the ultimate game of life —an ideal match for coaching.

One day, the moment came to share my vision with a local golf pro. He liked my ideas and our discussion revealed interesting possibilities. Feeling no need to strategize, I let go... leaving shortly thereafter for a month-long trip to Africa. On my return, I found a lengthy article in the newspaper promoting our upcoming workshop. As if guided by an invisible hand, the idea kept evolving. The first six-week program was enriched with participants who brought new opportunities. I distinctly felt part of something much bigger than my willpower alone could create; I learned to humbly be in the flow rather than fighting the current and the ball has kept rolling.

The more I simply am this presence of potential, the more I am aligned with what wants to happen. The times when I allow myself to be carried forward are the times when miracles happen, when potential translates into reality. The interdependency of being receptive and acting powerfully sometimes feels like a dance of masculine and feminine energies.

The intensity of these moments reminds me of my experience on Pushkin Square. It is the same feeling of being alive, of time slowing down... only now, this precious state is unthreatened by the fragile uncertainty of inner or outer worlds. No force is needed to maintain things a certain way. Success is no longer limited to a few occasions when everything finally becomes what I think it should be.

Knowing that I am part of what unites all of us has changed my perspective on my own importance—I feel both more insignificant and more responsible. As if things were at the same time more and less dependent on me. Currently, success to me is a way of being, allowing, accepting, embracing and dancing. Accepting what is has become a powerful stepping-stone from which I invite the future. I wonder what success means to you and how that definition impacts your perspective on life?

I THINK I CAN!

Denise N. Perez, New Jersey

*"I took in a slow, deep breath. My
personal quest to achieve a previously
inconceivable goal had finally begun."*

Growing up, I was not particularly athletic.
In fact, throughout my school years gym
class often struck fear in my heart, leaving
me with an unwelcome level of anxiety. I was afraid to
play kickball, dodge ball, softball, volleyball, and pretty
much any sport involving a ball for fear of getting hit
and painfully injured. Whenever the ball headed toward me, panic would seize my body, causing my eyes
to involuntarily shut, my hands to tightly clench, and
my body to preemptively flinch as I braced myself for
the worst.

However, even more than having to participate in
these sports, what I dreaded most about gym class was
the mandatory Presidential Physical Fitness Test that
taunted me every spring. The one-mile run was especially challenging because running more than a few
minutes produced horrible pains in my sides and left me
desperately gasping for air. My best efforts amounted to

little more than a snail's scurry, so I never finished the one-mile run in the time required to be deemed "physically fit." In fact, in all my years of school, not once did I pass the Presidential Physical Fitness Test! So I think it's safe to say that I was never "Ms. Athletic."

In all fairness, there were other things I was really good at like math, science, writing, and even dancing. But that didn't change the fact that my athleticism left much to be desired. Given my less than lustrous track record in sports, I quite often began telling myself, "I can't: I can't run, I can't swim, I can't do this and I can't do that." Little did I know that each time I told myself I couldn't do something, I was actually perpetuating my inability to do it.

In my late twenties, I was introduced to the concept that we create our lives with our own thoughts and beliefs. This concept is built on the premise that our thoughts create our feelings, our feelings prompt our actions, and our actions determine our life outcomes. If this concept holds true, then it would mean in each and every moment, we'd literally have the opportunity to create something new. Regardless of whatever happened in the past, we'd have the ability to construct a new life for ourselves simply by changing our thoughts.

Naturally, I was a little skeptical at first, but open-minded enough to consider there might be something to it. So I decided to register for the Nike Run Hit Wonder 10K event despite the fact that running had been such a miserably painful struggle for me in school. I knew this 6.2 mile challenge would surely test my resolve and had the potential to be a mind-blowing, life-changing experience if I were to actually finish the race.

Step one was to change my negative, defeatist thinking. I quickly replaced all of the "I can'ts" with "I cans." I made a commitment to myself to finish the race. For support, I asked a friend of mine, an avid runner, to help me train. For the next four months, I trained regularly, making it a point to run at least three times per week. At first, running half a mile was quite a stretch, leaving me panting and begging for air. But I slowly worked my way up to 1 mile, then 1.5 miles, 2 miles, 3 miles, and finally 4 miles. Without having even run the race, I was already in awe of my progress.

For those that have run a marathon before, a 10K might sound like a stroll in the park. However, in my mind, a 10K was equivalent to Forrest Gump's cross-country run, which lasted 3 years, 2 months, 14 days, and 16 hours (each way)!

When the day of the event finally arrived, I was quite nervous because, in all of my training, I had never actually run the complete 10 kilometers. Up to that point, 4 miles had been the longest distance I had run in my entire life! But, with my new positive attitude, I was determined to cross that finish line, no matter what!

With hundreds of people of all ages and walks of life gathered near the starting line, a loud bang marked the beginning of the race. I took in a slow, deep breath. My personal quest to achieve a previously inconceivable goal had finally begun. The 6.2 miles that stood between me and that finish line were my only concern, and although there were numerous runners around me, they all quickly faded away as I began running at a slow and steady pace.

I wish I could say that once the race began, time flew by and the 10 kilometers were completely painless, but that would be a lie. The truth is, there were moments when my body felt so fatigued it was screaming for me to stop. My mind tried to conjure up ways I could give myself a respectable "out" and not have to complete the race. It said things like, "You don't have to prove anything to anyone!" and "What's really the point of being able to run 10 kilometers anyway? It's not like anybody ever gets chased by wild buffalo these days!" These thoughts weren't helpful. They were only trying to stop me from reaching a goal I had set for myself. So I quickly began to create more supportive and encouraging thoughts. There were times I felt like the Little Engine that Could, repeating, "I think I can, I think I can, I think I can…" I simply refused to stop.

By the time I crossed the finish line, the event was pretty much over. Most of the bands that had been performing on the stages set up at the mile markers had already packed up their equipment and left. Volunteers were in the clean-up mode, picking up trash and breaking down the tables used for water stations along the running path. Needless to say, I was one of the last ones to finish the race.

Yet that didn't matter to me. What mattered was that I did something I previously thought I couldn't do, and I never gave up. With aching joints and indescribable pains that made it challenging to walk with any kind of normalcy, I took in a deep breath and spent a moment truly appreciating my personal victory. Tears quietly streamed down my cheeks as I grasped the magnitude of what had just happened. Never ever again could I say, "I can't run."

Thoughts and beliefs are extremely powerful, for they literally create our lives. I lived my life believing that I couldn't run when all along I was capable of finishing an entire 10K race with some training and steadfast determination. This experience taught me an incredibly valuable lesson. If you strive for things that seem out of reach, you just might be surprised at what you can actually achieve. More importantly, if you want to do something or be something more than you ever thought possible, you must challenge your current ways of thinking and consciously choose thoughts and beliefs that support you in achieving your goals.

THE ART OF LIVING
Becky Rothstein, Israel

*"I renounced guilt trips by choosing
my responses to life."*

"I am as I am—how wonderful!" I feel good,
happy, balanced and flowing with Life. I
am in a beautiful paradise resort in the
Carmel Forest of northern Israel leading the teacher-
training workshop called, "Love Yourself, Heal Your
Life." The participants are presenting their projects
to the group and my heart sings! I have grown so! But
it wasn't always that way.

It all started in Chile, where I was born to a wonderful, caring Dutch family. My father immigrated to Chile
in 1939; my mother's family perished in the Holocaust,
leaving her alone in this huge world. My paternal grandfather found Mother in Sweden through the Red Cross
and brought her to Chile. As a child I loved to hear the
story of how my father fell in love with her upon seeing
her picture. They married less than a year later. My
soul chose this loving environment to experience life
and grow.

As a child I felt everything was special. I remember being full of joy and self-esteem, creating happiness around me. I was an actor, dancer, musician and painter. I wanted it all! I remember my excitement when I first fell in love, dancing on the rooftop and feeling beautiful.

At age eleven I contracted polio, or perhaps meningitis. I remember my father carrying me all the way downstairs to an easy chair. I sat there waiting for friends who never came because of their fear of contagion. The experience of learning to walk again has been erased from my consciousness...or has it really? So many times I walk, *knowing* I will fall, though I don't. Where does this apprehension originate? I remember every starting point in my life being frightening—walking, starting school, a new job, a relationship.

When I was sixteen, my parents decided to move to Israel where most of our family lived. The difference in mentality, the harsh Hebrew language, and the religious school in Tel Aviv that was so dull in comparison with the beautiful, colorful instruction I had known in Chile, were almost impossible hurdles to overcome.

I unconsciously began to stifle my creativity. I perceived a world of fear, difficulty, non-acceptance and judgment. Where did that joyful girl disappear? I learned to give the world what I thought it wanted. The idea, "What do they expect from me?" became my closest companion. It was painful as I unconsciously created a deep ache where my insecurities grew.

At age thirty I found myself a neurotic, unhappy wife and mother, angry at the universe, presenting myself to the world as a good homemaker, mother and daughter, just as I was supposed to be. The pain of my childhood illness came back to haunt me after all those years. My cells remembered. It was time for my body to express itself.

After the birth of our youngest daughter 23 years ago my body experienced an earthquake. My right leg started to shorten, I suffered terrible back pains, and my stomach revolted against the constant pain medication I took. I was so young and so crippled.

However, when the student is ready the teacher appears. I started to explore various healing modalities. After some practice, in 1999 I was truly ready to CHANGE. I wanted to release the fear and learn to trust God and myself. I traveled all the way from Tel Aviv to San Diego to participate in a life training course with Dr. Patricia Crane based on the philosophy of Louise Hay in her book, *You Can Heal Your Life*. When I returned home only 10 days later, I was a different person. I renounced guilt trips by choosing my responses to life. I learned I could decide what to think, and instructed my chattering mind, "Don't give it another thought."

My life transformed itself. I could change, and I knew it deep inside. Images of tripping and falling have faded. Today if I experience pain I work on loving myself and the pain goes. For more than ten years I've been free of medication. I walk erect now without limping. Life is wonderful, even with its challenges, because my perspective has changed completely.

The work never ends. I am always at *Bereshit*, the Hebrew term for Genesis, the beginning of all times. It will never be done, and I enjoy the journey. I counter any feelings of insecurity by emulating my lovely mother who started over entirely after the Holocaust, marrying and bringing children, grand children and great grandchildren to this world. Yes, it can be done! We are constantly creating, and it's not frightening anymore.

Today, when I am fearful in my mind, I choose to think a different thought that brings me peaceful feelings. We have a wonderful place in the South of Israel on the Red Sea called Eilat. When I am in a dark corner within myself I imagine the beautiful beach there with the crystal waters, and I sooth myself to create inner peace. When I look at this beautiful, scared soul within me, I feel so much love for my inner child and great connection to God.

It took me only two weeks after the San Diego training to begin teaching in Israel. A few more workshops with Patricia enabled me to quit working at our family plant and dedicate myself to teaching Love. Many years before, I had studied and practiced interior decoration for homes. Today I decorate souls.

It is an honor and privilege to teach others how to transform their lives. Tears of joy and gratitude spring to my eyes for the participants in my workshops. They are my pearls, an awesome feeling. Although there are many healing stories from them, I will share two with you.

One wonderful woman came to me for help in releasing her need for anger. She had controlling parents who had created distance between her and her son. She was also going through a difficult time at work where one of her employees wanted to establish her own competitive endeavor. She cried and released a lot at the workshop until she was cleansed. In the evening, we gathered to celebrate her birthday, preparing a birthday tree with our good wishes. In the midst of the party, the door opened and in walked her parents and coworker with a big cake and even bigger smiles. We had experienced a miracle. She had released her anger and the Universe responded with love.

Another woman, a friend named Asnat, suffered with fibromyalgia. She had participated in one of my workshops some time ago, but after only three meetings she quit. Confronting her issues was so painful for her that after each meeting she suffered terrible pains in her body. However, when she was ready she called me to attend the upcoming workshop. Asnat arrived filled with anger and, as one of the participants put it, returned home as if she had been cleansed in a washing machine full of fabric softener. I was deeply moved. I knew we all had changed with her as she went through her work of light, starting with forgiveness. Through her we all found those places in ourselves where more love was needed. She got many hugs from us all, perhaps enough to last a lifetime! I felt blessed to be present. She had marshaled all her power and courage just to survive, and now she used it to heal herself, body and soul.

My intention and prayer today is to spread these wonderful tools of healing around the globe. I do my part here in Israel while other lamp workers extend their love and light wherever it is welcome so we can all heal this wonderful, unique planet in which we live.

Amen

TAKING RESPONSIBILITY FOR
MY REFLECTION

Rozana Gilmore, Nevada

*"If each experience in life is a reflection of
thoughts, words and feelings, what good will it
do to polish the mirror instead of the inner self?"*

By the time I was in my mid-thirties my relationships with men had become so overwhelming that I made a decision never to get involved with one ever again. For the most part my relationships were unfulfilling at best, toxic and abusive at their worst. Whether it was someone new or a long time friendship developing a romantic spark, I seemed doomed when it came to matters of the heart. Every "outlaw renegade bad-boy" without a prayer of making a commitment was attracted to me. I was an equal opportunity bum magnet.

Over the years I sought ways to create a better life and a successful relationship. I read books, went to lectures, learned meditation and visualization. I did get results each time I tried something new, however, I would eventually backslide ending up not quite where I started, but certainly not where I wanted to be. There were one or two men who had some redeeming qualities along the way, but that was it and it just never seemed to work out.

Then I came across an article by Daisaku Ikeda about how our lives are reflected back not just in physical form when we look into a mirror, but in every experience and relationship we have. This "clear mirror" concept awakened me to the realization that there was no reason for me to be frustrated with my present circumstances. They were only a reflection of my inner self. My experiences had been showing me, to myself! A tarnished and dingy reflection revealed my true beliefs and thoughts about men, relationships and everything else in my life. I realized that if my experiences in life are a reflection of my thoughts, words and feelings, what good will it do to polish the mirror instead of my inner self?

I took a painful look at all my past relationships and how I felt about my life to find the clues as to how and why this continued to happen. It didn't take long to see how I had unknowingly sabotaged myself. I realized love, from my perspective, equaled: *I don't have time for you; you are not important* or *go away and stop bothering me.* This was the stuff cluttering up my inner self. Being left alone is what I was programmed for, and I always ended up in that same place. My earliest experiences formed my opinions and thoughts, and those same opinions and thoughts were now forming my experiences.

The women I knew had sacrificed everything for their relationships and family while the men did what they pleased, when they pleased, and with whom they pleased. Wives and children were left to settle for what crumbs of time or affection were thrown to them, if any. I felt invisible, ignored, and unlovable and that's what was mirrored back to me time and time again. Each relationship confirmed those feelings. No matter how much I polished the mirror, there was my inner self reflecting back at me. My results matched my beliefs!

Whether consciously or subconsciously, my thoughts, words and fears condemned me to a life full of everything I didn't want.

I was so encouraged by the "clear mirror" article I wanted to polish the mirror of my inner self to see the reflection I desired. Unsure of how to make these changes at first, I started by looking at what I didn't want in my life any longer. Even these seemingly harmless thoughts made people from my past resurface. I knew at that point I had to focus on what I did want, keeping all other thoughts out of my mind and these guys out of my life. It took a little time in the beginning, especially since I had no real role models for a healthy relationship or a basis for comparison. What I got from the article was so intriguing I could not stop thinking about it. And with the past resurfacing for a brief moment when I focused on what I didn't want I knew there was something to this. I was compelled to put the concept to the test.

Within 30 days of reading the article and paying close attention to my thoughts and feelings, three men came into my life. The first is married to a woman who had broken her neck as a teenager and is a quadriplegic. He admires her and is totally devoted to their marriage. The second was reading Mars/Venus and trying to get his wife to work on their relationship and go to counseling (completely the opposite of anything I had ever known). The third was a man who seemed abrasive and unapproachable. He was a teacher I was assigned to help at the school where I worked. He saw me shivering from the air conditioning in class one day and came over to put his jacket over my shoulders; a side of him I'd not seen before surfaced. Hmmm? Men like this in my environment, what a switch. My inner self caught a glimpse of a new reflection. It was clear to me that what I think about and how I feel makes a difference in my life and for everyone around me.

A short time later I met a wonderful man named Joseph. We have now been married for eight years. We see in each other the reflection of our inner selves.

The awareness of who I want to be and what I want to attract has allowed me to heal my past and take responsibility for what I create. Every area of my life now reflects the changes I have made. My health, finances and relationships continue to get better and better.

Lengendary Luncheon
Tammy S. Blankenship, Ohio

"Inspired by Oprah, I wanted to find a way to
host my own "luncheon" to honor the men, women
and children who have enhanced my journey."

Last year, Oprah Winfrey hosted a "Legends Ball." In her magazine, when describing how the event came to be, Oprah said, "I started thinking about all the women who'd come before me, many of whom have now passed on—women whose steps created a journey of no boundaries for my generation. I wanted to thank them, celebrate them, and rejoice in their spirit." Inspired by Oprah, I wanted to find a way to host my own "luncheon" to honor the men, women and children who have enhanced *my* journey.

Welcome to Tammy's Legend Luncheon

Everything is in place. I have spared no expense for my important guests! Tables covered in fine linen, scattered under a canopy, sparkle with multi-colored

Fiesta dinnerware and mismatched, beautiful glasses. No two place settings are alike and nothing matches. How liberating! Candles grace every table, accented with flowered candle rings and baskets of multicolored roses. Jimmy Buffett's latest album urges everyone to kick off his or her sandals and dance!

Before any guests arrive, I check in with "chef" Donnie, the wonderful man I am dating, to make sure the grilled crab legs, strip steaks and lobster tails are ready to broil. Fresh-picked corn on the cob is bubbling in a riot of yellow and white. The baked potatoes are ready and begging for a slathering of sour cream and butter. Cindy's Japanese Chicken Salad is chilled and ready for her famous dressing. I am so excited by how wonderful everything looks; I have to take a moment to kiss the chef!

Everyone is finally seated and I look around at the most important and influential people in my life. Each one helped create my "journey of no boundaries." Enormous waves of gratitude flood over me. I sincerely thank each of them for being in my life.

My two sons are sitting on each side of me; I thank them both for their innocence and their enthusiasm. Gabriel is the oldest and I appreciate his protective nature and his kind heart. Michael, my youngest, is trying to make all the other guests laugh at his impersonations and I am reminded of how I love his creativity.

Michael insisted that he sit next to "Poppy" and my Dad was happy to oblige him. My Dad is a living example of beauty and resilience. One of the things I love the most about my Dad is that he is admirable. I am proud of him and he inspires me everyday with his ability to make the best of things and do what is right, even when it's hard. Next to my Dad is his girlfriend. I love that my Dad has someone who loves him and takes care of him when he is sick. I love that she makes him happy.

Dixie is the next honored guest. Dixie hired me fresh out of college and became my mentor and friend. I am thankful to Dixie for believing in me even before I "had a clue!" With that belief, she inspired me to do an excellent job, incessantly reminding me that I was capable of accomplishing anything I desired!

Dr. D'iorio from Kent State is seated next to Dixie. Dr. D'iorio is my angel of ethics and I keep a picture of him in my office to remind me to do what my heart tells me to do with clients. When I am tangled up in bureaucracy, I look at his picture and ask myself what is best for the client. Dr. D'iorio inspires me to believe in, and strive for, the way things *should* be.

Half way around the table, directly across from me, is "chef" Donnie. Of course, he offered to cook for me today, as he fully participates in anything that is important to me. Since my Mom died, he has become my biggest fan. He encourages me, believes in me, gets his hands dirty helping me, keeps my car running and holds me when I am scared or tired. He does all of that and much more. I love and appreciate him more than words can say.

Next to Donnie are two empty chairs. The first one is an honorary place setting for Mom. She was busy in heaven and couldn't attend, but her spirit is always with us. Mom gave me an independent spirit and a backbone. I love her and miss her very, very deeply and I thank her for giving me life. The second empty chair is for Grandma Sweetie, who died a year after Mom. I thank my Grandma Sweetie for loving me and being the best person I ever met in my life.

My next guest is my first love. I thank him for being present for our two boys and making it possible for us to parent together, even though we are apart. I am grateful that we work together every day, focusing on what they need, not what we want. He inspired me by giving me the freedom to grow wings. I am honored by the past we share and the endless ways we will work to make our children happy in the future.

Aunt Katie occupies the next seat and she has shown me love my whole life. I thank Katie for everything from taking me on vacations with her when I was young, to staying at the hospital during Mom's last days. I am grateful for Katie's beautiful voice and her willingness to give away her last slice of bread to a stranger in need.

My co-workers occupy the next several chairs. Cindy inspires me to make things look good and have a lot of fun in life. I appreciate Michelle's honesty and her soft heart under the tough exterior. Billa inspires me with her patience and her quiet strength. I thank Robin for bringing some organization into my life and Jennifer for making me laugh out loud everyday. Cora's great attitude and love of the Lord is infectious and I love her for that. Much more than co-workers, these are cherished friends.

As everyone leans back into their chairs, full and satisfied, I thank them for joining me today. We have fresh strawberry pie for desert and everyone takes turns talking about what we are grateful for. We all talk about how much we miss Mom and Grandma, offering a special toast up to heaven. As a parting gift, each guest receives a lifetime supply of my love, admiration and respect.

I encourage you to host your own luncheon today. Find a comfortable place to sit where it is quiet for a while; while reflecting, you can plan the whole affair. The more details you can think of, the more meaningful it will be. Plan the place settings, the guest list and the menu. Finally, don't forget the music that inspired *you*!

After you plan and create the perfect day, recite all that you are thankful for. You will be inspired to invite these people to share a meal with you; during that time, express your gratitude to each honored guest for their special contribution to your life.

Anyone who is willing to share the story of his or her "luncheon" may send it to me at: tblankenship@ creatingsuccessstories.com.

BE CAREFUL WHAT YOU
WISH FOR . . .
Teresa Mills, Australia

*"I can't wait...I'll go to hospital and get
to sleep for a week and have the nurses
fuss over me – it will be wonderful!"*

Darren was a man who hated his job. He was an executive manager at a major bank and he desperately wanted a change but somehow just couldn't create one.

Instead of waking up every morning ready to enjoy life, he woke up dreading the day ahead. Although I didn't know it at the time, it got to the stage that part of his daily routine was to repeat to himself, "I wish I could be sick, so I could stay home and spend time with Teresa and be able to take the kids to school." All he wanted was a cold, or to bang his big toe – anything that would take him out of the office for a few days. What he got, however, was something else entirely . . .

At the time he suffered badly with blocked ears. Whenever he got a cold he would go deaf for up to three weeks—he couldn't hear anything, not even the children calling him. After a particularly bad cold, he finally went to the doctor who told him that he needed grommets put into his ears. This would help his ears to heal and help him to hear clearly.

Darren came out of the doctor's surgery telling me that the operation was set for the 7th of July. At that point my whole body went into a panic—"Why the 7th, why not the 6th or 8th. Why the 7th ?" But he simply said, "As soon as the doctor said the 7th, I was agreeing even before he had finished speaking, it just has to be the 7th. But don't worry, nothing is going to happen!" Famous last words.

The night before the operation, I had such a strong feeling that something was going to happen and was very stressed about this whole situation. We spoke about it, but he told me that everything would be fine and that I worried way too much. I'll never forget what he said next—"I can't wait, I'll go to hospital, get to sleep for a week and have the nurses fuss over me, it will be wonderful!" I didn't realise how accurate this prophecy would be until much later.

On the morning of the operation as they were wheeling him down to theatre, I had the strongest urge to say "Don't go!", but I thought what reason could he use? "Sorry Doc, not today—my wife feels funny!" So instead I said nothing.

The operation went smoothly with no problems at all. Then in recovery, the anaesthetist took out his breathing tube and at that point everything went wrong!

For some reason Darren coughed and his vocal chords spasmed causing some acid from his stomach to flow into his lungs. Damaged by the acid, his lungs filled with fluid and he quickly lost oxygen, his colour changing from pink to black in less than 30 seconds. It took six people to hold him down and another four to put the tube back down his throat because his body was convulsing so much.

One by one his bodily functions shut down. His body followed the perfect sequence of events to save oxygen. It was as if God had designed a perfect plan to save his brain and his body was following this plan to the letter. However, we were blessed that the four best senior intensive care specialists in the area all happened to be at the hospital at the same time, all able to work on keeping him alive.

They certainly had their work cut out for them as his kidneys had shut down, his heart was enlarged, his stomach, bowel and pancreas had shut down, and his liver was under a lot of pressure. And of course there were his lungs so filled with fluid that it literally was pouring out of his mouth—and then his sore ears.

With so many things wrong with him, the doctors didn't believe he would make it through the night, and quietly suggested I call the priest. Refusing to believe that he would leave his three beautiful girls (as he called us), I agreed to the priest giving him a blessing. Nothing more! I wasn't about to admit defeat and I knew that Darren wasn't either.

That night was the longest of my life. As the night wore on the priest failed to arrive, literally from next door, despite being called three times. I took it as a sign that we did not need his services and that Darren would survive, even if the doctors did not agree.

Going home to tell our two children that the person they loved the most in the whole world may have to go and be an angel was the hardest thing I have ever had to do, and a challenge I didn't think myself capable of until that moment. Jessica, who was five at the time, had just learnt the Hail Mary at school and together with three year old Lauren, we started to pray, and pray.

Thankfully for all of us, we were blessed with a miracle, and Darren survived. What's more he didn't sustain any long term damage to his body at all, and the recovery period was less than half what the doctors predicted.

As it happened he did sleep for a week, they had him in a drug induced coma for seven days! As for the nurses fussing over him, well, in intensive care, that's an understatement. And he did get to be off work for two months, he even got to take the kids to school!

Any person involved who did not believe God existed knew better by the end of this experience— family, friends, and even total strangers.

Some weeks later, Darren told me about his morning wish routine, lucky for him I didn't put him back into the hospital!

It was amazing that he was able to create this chain of events simply by thinking the same thought over and over. If such real and tangible results can be created with negative thoughts, imagine what wonderful things could be created with positive ones!

I guess the moral of the story is as the old adage goes: "Be careful what you wish for, you might just get it." So if you are going to wish for something, take it from me, make it something wonderful.

EGYPT:
HOW THE DREAM CAME TRUE
Norma Georgina Rodríguez Paz, Mexico

*"But I got a lesson from Nature and the incredible
power of the mind about how you can reach
your dreams no matter how high they are."*

On June 21st, 1995 I was flying from Mexico
City to Barajas Airport in Madrid, Spain
with a new friend, Sara María Esparza, a
girl I met recently in my English class at the office. I
just couldn't believe our final destination for this trip:
Egypt. Together, we are reaching our common dream
to visit Egypt.

I had waited more than 20 years to live this moment. When I was just a tiny girl on vacation in my aunt
Olivia's house, she got a postal card from Egypt. I didn't
know how to read, so I asked her about the wonderful
place in the photo. It was as if I had been there before.
She explained to me that was the gorgeous Sphinx in a
deep blue sky and the desert sand. Maybe that was the
moment that I fell in love with Egypt. I promised myself
to go there someday.

But as an adult I began to think it was going to be
very difficult to achieve this dream. Egypt is very far away

37

from Mexico. The trip would be quite expensive! What if traveling so far could be dangerous? Other similar ideas came to my mind. I began to think of this like a beautiful dream that would stay just a dream.

Even several months before my travel to Egypt, I still thought it wasn't possible to go there. But I got a lesson from Nature and the incredible power of the mind about how you can reach your dreams no matter how high they are.

One day, I was reading one of my Dad's books, about how our thoughts can influence our life. The book proposed a very simple exercise to prove it. I liked that because I've always been very skeptical. It said that you just need several beans and two containers. One container would have a letter "A", the other one a letter "B". Each container should have 10 beans, with some cotton balls and plenty of water at the bottom. This was the first part of the experiment.

Then in a very random way, I had to choose a container for the focus of my positive thoughts. I used the worldwide method of flipping a coin and it came up for container B. Next I had to hide both containers, even from me, and not tell anyone about the experiment. For the next 15 days I just had to think about my beautiful beans in container B and how they became wonderful beans plants: tall, plenty of life, strong, and lovely. I also sent love to them and visualized them growing up. These thoughts were made several times each day.

It didn't take 15 days to do this, because about two days before the due date, something "green" and tall appeared at the top of the shelf where I hid the containers. They were the bean plants in container B. My lovely plants! They reached about 7 times taller than the ones in container A. I just couldn't believe it!

Then I realized, if my thoughts affected my plants this way, imagine every time that I say "it's not possible to reach my dream," I am making it a big truth. I am creating my future with every thought that crosses my mind in the now.

So I changed and began to affirm, "Now I am traveling to Egypt. Everything is perfect. I am enjoying the time of my life. I have the perfect company on this trip. People are so kind and I am perfectly safe. I have enough money for all my needs, and plenty of time to visit this country."

I opened my mind to accept the perfect person to share the dream, and the perfect time. I began to exchange pesos for US dollars, because the travel price would change less in that currency. And most important of all: I did believe it was possible. I was accepting my responsibility in making this true. A big lesson came from small beans.

One day in my job, I met Sara Maria in the English class. Somebody told me she really loved to travel to several places in the world. I thought, *maybe she hasn't gone to Egypt yet.* So I asked her. "Have you ever been in Egypt?"

"No," she said, "but I would like to. It is as if that place is calling me."

"Well," I replied, "I was considering going there this year." With excitement, she said, "Amazing! Why don't we go together?" I didn't even have to ask her to go! She told me that a sister of hers was living in Spain and could get better prices for the trip if we went there first.

Without even asking, again she told me, "If you need money there, count on me and you can pay me later." However, I discovered the company had loans for employees, so I got all the money that I needed. Next challenge: I was new to the company and didn't have enough vacation days for the trip. But I was able to negotiate with the company to give me the extra time without pay. Everything was coming together!

Then my parents were worried about the travel. They expressed all the "what if...?" questions. I had never been so far from them, and without any member of the family. I tried to convince them I had to be there. It was a lifetime dream.

Sara began to have doubts about the trip, and her family was worried. When she suggested postponing the trip for a year, I said no. I really wanted to go Egypt then. I was going to get married the next year, and wasn't sure if I'd have another opportunity. I thought, *it is now or never. If she can't go with me, maybe I should go on my own.* Luckily, Sara changed her mind and decided to come with me.

Before we left, my friends at the office gave me beautiful sunglasses "for the Sahara Desert". They said they'd never seen someone so happy about travel. It was because it was not, "just a travel" but that I was making my *dream* come true.

Finally, when we were flying to Spain, I just couldn't believe this was happening. At last!

In Spain we visited the Egypt Embassy to get our Egyptian visa. A few days later, we were landing in Cairo. We went directly to the boat at the Nile River, the longest river in the world. I had that sensation that people call *deja vú*. Sara felt the same. It was like coming home after a long absence. Sailing along the Nile was wonderful.

People were so gentle everywhere. Families asked us to be in their photographs. We were treated like queens. We visited the great pyramids at Giza, precious statues, huge obelisks, and heard all about the Pharaohs and the greatest times of this amazing country. Even the market with its colors and smells was wonderful. Of course, one of the most beautiful monuments we saw was the Sphinx. Just imagine how many, many years it has been there!

There are not enough words to express how wonderful it was to see my dream becoming a reality. Each of us even had marriage proposals there! But most important of all, I learned I can use my mind to create the life I want. Sometimes I have the tendency to forget this huge truth, but my bean plants showed me I could reach my biggest dream then, so now I continue having bigger dreams and making them all my reality.

A DREAM COME TRUE
Lisa K. Story, California

*"Had I ignored the possibilities along
the journey, I would have passed up the
opportunity to live out my dream."*

All of us have hopes, dreams and visions for our lives. The key is to make those possibilities realities. Many great spiritual teachers speak about the power of intention and the power of our thoughts. I believe that we must continually ask ourselves the question, "What is the life I dream for myself?" I still feel gleefully tickled and amazed each time I see my intentions manifest into a reality. Having my dreams turn into realities reminds me in such a direct way how powerful my thoughts and my intentions really are.

Almost nine years ago, I attended a Heal Your Life Teacher training in beautiful San Diego. Near the end of the week-long workshop we had the joy of being entertained by a very funny and talented musician by the name of Scott Kalechstein. One of Scott's songs is called *Say Yes to Your Dreams!* One evening he performed this song for us and invited workshop participants to come up one at a time and exuberantly declare a personal dream as he took a break in the song. After each participant declared their dream, Scott would enthusiastically begin playing again and singing with all the other people in the audience the line in the chorus which was "Say yes to your dreams!"

It was quite the positive affirmation for all who participated. After watching several people get up and do this, I nervously took the plunge, jumped up and shouted out my very secret dream, "I want to perform on stage in a musical!" Scott and the rest of the participants sang joyfully, "Say yes to your dreams!" affirming my hearts desire. I sat down feeling a little foolish and self-conscious about declaring my aspiration to perform on stage, particularly when I didn't sing. I had been told numerous times over the years that I couldn't carry a tune and I would make fun of myself good-naturedly. So, even though I loved singing, I only sang privately in my car where no one else could hear me. I had never sung in public and always mouthed the *Happy Birthday* song whenever faced with that situation. The point is my dream seemed to be a pretty far-fetched dream and I was feeling silly for having mentioned it. At any rate, it was a fun evening in San Diego. The workshop ended and I went back home.

A few months later, my seven year-old daughter, Sydney, brought home a flyer from school promoting different activities and extracurricular classes that were being offered for children in our community. We looked through it and she decided she wanted to try musical theater classes. We signed her up and twice a week we went to the local theater for classes. At the end of the first series, Sydney's acting teacher announced that the theater was planning to perform the children's musical *The Velveteen Rabbit.* Auditions would be held for all children interested. My daughter was very enthusiastic about wanting to do it so we went to the auditions. As I sat there watching all of the children auditioning, I learned that there were a handful of adult roles in the show. I felt a little stir of excitement brewing at the possibility of an opportunity. I inquired as to how the adult roles would be cast and was told "through auditions, just like the kids." I rationalized with my fearful self that I might as well audition, because if I was going to be driving Sydney to rehearsals, it would make sense that I would be in the show also.

After watching all of the children audition, they finally got to those few adult roles. I very hesitantly told the director that I would like to audition. With a serious case of butterflies in the stomach and a load of adrenaline shooting through my veins, I auditioned singing the only song I knew by heart, *From a Distance*, originally performed by Bette Midler.

It would be an understatement to say that my daughter and I were very excited when we learned both of us had been given roles in the musical. Going through the process of rehearsals and performing on stage with my daughter was an experience I will never forget. It was fantastic, marvelous and exhilarating all at the same time. Shortly after the show closed, I auditioned for another musical and was given a part. The entire experience was more than I could have ever imagined. It brought so much joy and helped me to feel more confident in myself. My entire life I had secretly dreamed of performing on stage, but until I powerfully and publicly stated my intention it never became a reality. In fact, it never even crossed my mind that it could be a reality.

I learned a valuable lesson that year about intention and how we manifest our dreams. Not only must we put our intentions out into the universe, but it is just as important to pay attention to the signs leading us to our dreams and then acting upon those signs regardless of our fears and anxieties. Had I ignored the possibilities along the journey, I would have passed up the opportunity to live out my dream. Had I given into the fear of singing in front of others or the fear of looking foolish I would not have lived my dream.

There are many, many ways we can deliver our intentions. One year I made a list of my dreams. Just a simple list of things I hoped for or things I hoped to achieve. There were approximately 100 items on the list, some big and some small. I forgot about the list and found it in a box a few years later. I discovered that I had achieved 67 dreams on the list! This simple action turned into a ritual that I perform at the beginning of each year. I review my list at the end of the year to see how many of my intentions have manifested into realities. I also have a dream board that hangs in my kitchen on the face of my refrigerator. I cut out pictures, quotes and words or anything that interests me and seems worthy of my dream board. I add to it anytime I run across something else I desire. Because it's on my refrigerator, I see it frequently. The results of these processes are amazing. Our thoughts and visualizations are powerful and the power seems to magnify when we pull our dreams out of the hidden recesses of our mind and declare them out loud to the universe in one form or another.

Incidentally, my own personal dream board includes a phrase I cut out of a magazine that depicted a lifelong dream of mine to write. It was the phrase, "me write book." Two weeks after pasting the statement onto my dream board, I received the invitation to participate in this book!!! As the saying goes, "Be careful what you wish for!" Your dreams just may come true.

ON TURNING FIFTY

Irene Humbach, New York

*"I look in the mirror at fifty years that
seem to have passed in the blink of an
eye, and I struggle to take it in."*

After fifty years of being in this life, there is
one thing I know I am good at—getting
people to tell their stories. Every day, as
a holistic therapist and healer, I receive their stories,
sensing the earnestness with which they yearn for a
vessel to hold their truth.

Sometimes, perhaps even often, I am not such
a pure vessel. I come and listen anyway, knowing instinctively that too pure a vessel would not allow us to
connect, to hold sacred, the human experience. I have
been through a lot in my life—hopes, dreams, love, loss,
success, failure, pain, joy—even one moment of bliss that
has become the cornerstone of my spirituality. While
most days present a murky mixture of all the above and
more, it is my growing belief that this is the place where
we connect; where, in sharing our vulnerabilities and our
everyday heroism, we come a bit more to know who we
are, and why we are here. Then we transcend the isola-

tion that keeps us separate and we come to savor more the mystery of our oneness.

My mother, who turns 80 this year as I turn 50, often tells me, "Irene, you should write a book!" This statement usually comes out of her when, yet again, I am making another change in my life. Since she has lived in the same two-family house for over 50 years, and was married to the same man for 43 years, my life must truly be a "puzzlement," as the King sang to Anna in the "King and I" when confronted with her unfamiliar ways. When I look back over 33 years since I flew to Nova Scotia to become a Sister of Charity at 17, knowing with the ruthless certainty afforded only to youth that this is what I would be doing for the rest of my life, I can only agree, "…tis a puzzlement!"

Professionally I have been teacher, administrator, pastoral counselor, community organizer, medical social worker, psychiatric social worker, employee assistance counselor, grief counselor, bioenergetic therapist, private practitioner, and most recently, energy healer. Personally, I have been nun, ex-nun, single woman, wife, step-mother, step-grandmother, divorcee, "significant other," as well as friend, colleague, daughter, granddaughter, sister, aunt. I have never been "mother" – an ache I admittedly feel deep in my heart and my womb as I cross the threshold of the "elder" and now know, for certain, that it will never be.

I have moved approximately 20 times in 33 years, learning to live lightly, mostly from my early training as a nun when I had two habits, two veils, two pairs of shoes, and a trunk, into which everything you owned was supposed to fit when you moved to a new assignment. I still have everything I own in a three-room condo and an office. I have never been a pack-rat, and try to have just what I need, and not a lot more. Clutter makes me nutty! I try to live debt-free (a lesson from my father), which to this day, I have been pretty much able to stick to.

Experiences, stories, connections that cannot be counted: these are my treasures. On bad days, I lose sight of all the people whose paths have mingled with mine, and I struggle with doubt about the purpose of my life. Currently, no house, no husband, no children or grandchildren, or large sums of money in the bank to define who I am. On good days, I nearly vibrate with the awareness of giver/receiver, healer/healee, becoming one and the same—over and over healing each other in the sharing of our stories. Such richness cannot be measured or put in a trunk to look at whenever I need validation! No, to touch this richness, I need simply remind myself to close my eyes and sit in stillness, allowing my energy and the energies of all who have been a part of my life to converge, once again, in the arena of spirit. When that happens, all doubts and questions gently, quietly dissolve . . . like mist in the morning sun.

I look in the mirror at 50 years that seem to have passed in the blink of an eye, and I struggle to take it in. How can I possibly be 50 years old! I still don't know who I want to be when I grow up! I need more time! Yet here I stand, ready or not, at the threshold of the "Elder," knowing only that there is one thing that I am really good at—getting people to tell their stories.

To all of you who have ever been a vessel for me, whether for a moment or a lifetime, I thank you. You know who you are. In the listening and the receiving of my story, you have allowed me to become me, and curiously, mysteriously, more: I have become you.

Some day, maybe, I *will* write that book—a story about stories and the power they hold to heal our hearts.

P.S. In 2003, I happily re-married at age 55, and now have a wonderful husband, home and four stepchildren to add to my riches . . . and my stories! Life is good!

THE GIFT OF THE INDIGO ANGEL

Rev. Lynn Collins, California

*"As I watched from my vantage point on the
ceiling, the most marvelous healing began."*

It was bright and sunny, not a cloud in the
blue San Diego sky. The temperature was just
the right degree of warm and the smell of the
earth was fresh and damp. What a glorious morning to
be out in the garden tending to the gay profusion of
flowers that graced the back yard. I was basking in the
delight of watching a pair of tiny, ruby throated hum-
ming birds gather their nectar when I was suddenly
overcome with the need to go into meditation. And I
had to do it now.

Sitting in the big, comfortable chair where I medi-
tated every morning, legs crossed and palms facing up-
wards, it took only a few seconds to join with the higher
energies. And then, in my minds eye, there appeared a
beautiful Indigo Blue Angel. She was tall and slender. A
silver halo glowed behind her long blue hair. The silver
beads of her necklace shown brightly against her flowing
blue robe which was tied at the waist with a silver cord.

Soft silver slippers adorned her feet and an iridescent blue light shimmered all around her.

We spoke telepathically. "Do you want to go somewhere with me?" she asked.

"Yes," I replied, "where are we going?"

"To do a special healing," she said. "You'll see."

Our hands joined and away we flew, entering a bright, midnight blue, night time sky. After a few minutes it was daylight again. The Indigo Angel shape-shifted into a stork, carrying me in a white cloth sling that hung from her beak. She was giving me clues but I still didn't know where we were going. We had started in California and were heading east. I looked down at the land below. It was lovely, like looking from a low flying plane only better. The topography was spectacular—colors, canyons, mountains, rivers, deserts and forests. I was so enthralled with the beauty of the earth below me that I hardly noticed our drop in altitude. Then, boom, the state of South Carolina loomed large before us.

The next thing I knew, we were looking through the ceiling of a room. There, lying sleeping on a bed, was my daughter-in-law. She was completely surrounded by Angels and Spirits. As I watched from my vantage point on the ceiling, the most marvelous healing began. Many bright blue etheric hands outlined in the brightest white light were gently laid upon her physical head and heart chakra. She was about six months pregnant at the time. More etheric hands were then gently and carefully opening her etheric belly. The baby was removed and handed into the care of a very large, stout black woman who was dressed in a white nurse's uniform covered by a red and white checkered apron. She held him very protectively throughout the healing.

The magical hands followed the geometrical grid of her body, adjusting here, adjusting there. Swift, quick, precise; firm, gentle and confident were the movements.

It was so exciting to see. I was frozen still and quiet and yet quite activated by the amazing spectacle that was taking place before me.

Then they were finished. The baby was ever so gently removed from the nurse's arms and put back into the womb. The etheric hands softly pushed the skin back over the belly, closing it, sort of melting it back together. Her blankets were put back in place and she lay there peacefully sleeping. As far as she knew, nothing had happened.

Physical awareness returned. I was back in my chair... feeling grateful ...the prayers had been answered.

This was a high risk pregnancy. Test results had shown the possibility of Downs Syndrome. The news was terribly upsetting to me. Reiki healing is my personal solution for everything. But when I tried sending Reiki to the situation, I couldn't. It was like I was short circuiting and the energy wouldn't flow. But something had to be done. I was on a Reiki healing telephone tree with at least fifteen other Reiki Masters. Whenever there was a need for healing the call was given to all of us. We, in turn, would call other Reiki practitioners and spread the request. I called the phone tree, contacted all my Reiki students and Reiki Circle participants. I called all the Science of Mind practitioners I personally knew and many of the local area churches to ask for Spiritual Mind Treatment, plus put the pregnancy on the prayer lists that are available through the Self-Realization Fellowship, Unity Churches and Arnold Patent spiritual support groups. Hundreds of people were involved in the healing prayer that went out to the Universe. When the child was born, he was perfectly healthy and continues to be. At the time of this writing he is 10 years old.

WHAT IS LOVE?

Eva-Maria Riegler, England

"Make yourself a present today: Forgive yourself!"

A few years ago I found my fundamental beliefs about life and love deeply shattered. I was overwhelmed with grief because I had lost the love of my life. My husband "found love" with another woman after we had lived together for 21 years. To me, our marriage had been a very happy one and I was in shock when he announced that he was going to end it.

At a friends house, where I had taken refuge to gather strength, I came across a book in which the Dalai Lama answered the question, "What is love?" The Dalai Lama explained that Hollywood style romantic love is unstable and moody, while true love is free of conditions. Applying the Dalai Lama's wisdom to my situation meant that if I truly loved my husband I would forgive him for letting his family down and wish him well. This felt puzzling. Even the Dalai Lama admitted that it is easier said than done to love those who annoy or hurt us.

My husband and I had lived together all my adult life. The thought of being without him seemed unbearable. I felt rejected and vulnerable and overwhelmed by fears about an uncertain future. The things I feared most were being unhappy and lonely, not being a good mother on my own, and not being able to cope with the demands of life. The suffering of our daughter who was only nine years old caused me even more pain. My husband had given a promise, he had a responsibility towards his family. How could I ever forgive him and let him get away with it? "I am not Mother Theresa for Christ's sake!", was my woeful cry; Love was buried under my fears.

A friend recommended that I start to meditate. Meditation helped me see more clearly and in the silence of meditation I was able to release my fears. Whenever I sat down to meditate I felt this sense of quiet and peace arising from within. It was like a purification of the heart, making me open and receptive to new thinking.

In my search for a way out of my misery I read many books which carried a key message: *We can decide to change! Fear is a belief in negative thoughts! Change the thoughts and the fear must go!* Well, that sounded too easy to be true. On the other hand I had nothing to lose if I tried.

I started with a few thought experiments and imagined myself in ten years time, having a wonderful, loving relationship with my daughter, enjoying the company of all my lovely friends, living with a wonderful new partner, working successfully in a fulfilling career, earning a great income, etc.

Amazingly these thoughts changed my feelings of misery instantly because they took away the fears I had about myself and my future. Of course my fears returned as soon as I finished my thought experiment, because old thinking patterns do not disappear over night. A bit like weeds, they have to be removed again and again. But what remained was the insight that emotional pain and anger are caused by fears! My misery had not come from my rejected love but from *my fearful reaction* to it! This insight was a breakthrough which changed my situation fundamentally.

I started to do positive affirmations, which means to think and write positive, loving thoughts. I learned this from Louise Hay, a metaphysical teacher whose books I cannot recommend highly enough. I told myself that 'I can do it,' that this experience will ultimately strengthen me and make me happier, and I do not need a partner to know that I am worth loving. I told myself that I am free, that I have nothing to fear, and that I am safe. I affirmed that my desire and foremost aim in life is to be a warm and gentle presence for my daughter and others and to be forgiving and compassionate. This was my new purpose. I began to trust that love is the only solution to all challenges.

All my life I have aimed for so many goals in the outer world to bring me happiness. But what had I done to polish my soul? What plans had I made to support the growing of my heart and learning to be more compassionate? Now I had the opportunity to do this.

I learned that meditation and affirming positive and loving thoughts are ways of focusing on love instead of allowing our ego to plant fear and thoughts of revenge, and this helps us grow and overcome obstacles. Instead of focusing on the wrong doings of my ex-partner I tried to see what was happening inside me. I concluded that my purpose in life was not ended by the dissolution of our marriage. On my mobile phone greeting, for instance, I am reminded every morning that "Everybody is doing the best they can. Love is our true reality. Fear is something our mind has made up. If somebody shows up today being unkind I will react with compassion."

I have to admit, of course, that I do not manage to practice these thoughts at all times, and I do not know anybody who does, but affirming the intention nevertheless keeps me going. It makes me happy to have found deep and meaningful aims which are totally independent of outer circumstances and give me more profound happiness.

One day in an art-gallery I came across an installation which said: "Make yourself a present today: Forgive yourself!" Suddenly I became aware that I was in the middle of learning to do exactly that! By looking in a loving and accepting way at my fears and all these thoughts of 'not being good enough' I was able to forgive myself for not being the wife my husband wanted me to be, for not being able to protect my daughter from the experience of divorce, and for victimising myself after the marriage ended. I released a lot of emotions by crying. Only then did I realize that I had also blamed myself for the end of our marriage and that there was a lot of guilt about my part in our relationship.

This was a liberating experience. Forgiving myself was not berating myself for having made mistakes, but accepting that I have done the best I could, with the knowledge and experience I had at the time. It dawned on me that this applies to all of us, without exception.

Gradually I could see that my ex-husband also did the best he could. He had only followed what he considered the path to his happiness. He had not intended to hurt anyone and he was suffering as well, I could see that. His hair had become even greyer and he had lost a lot of weight. Suddenly I became aware of a deep love and compassion towards him and all life around me; I felt deeply connected with life, more than ever before. It was as if a gate had opened—I felt free and strong and ready to start anew.

Yes, he has cut me out of his life and of course I am sad about the loss of my closest friend and ally, but beneath the scarred surface of our separated lives my love is undiminished and that gives me strength. The strength comes from the insight that love is bigger than we are, it is the core of our very existence. Even though Love is an invisible force, we can feel it very powerfully when we are aligned with it. Love inspires, renews and heals. It is there for all of us to share. By giving love we receive it! Often it is not until we encounter challenging situations and feel we have nothing left to hold on to that we finally reach out for the love that is always there. I am grateful that life has brought me such a challenge.

FINDING MY OWN VOICE

Caren M Kolerski, New York

*"My voice became suppressed as I
perceived that I had to be perfect..."*

Sitting quietly in meditation, I hear the sweet chirping of Spring beneath my window. Sparrows nestled within the evergreen bushes are singing their familiar songs, reminding me of earlier times as a young one in the nest with three younger sisters. A favorite pastime was chirping away to the Carpenters' songs on our old record player that Dad won as a milkman. I usually directed as each one sang her heart 'n soul out with collective dreams of becoming the next Lennon Sisters! I loved to sing and remember church choirs, high school glee club and a community chorus where we performed Handle's *Messiah*.

I inherited a beautiful soprano singing voice from my Mom, whose voice was of opera quality. As a child, however, I was often confused as I heard her voice more often shouting commands than singing sweet songs. By the time I was experiencing facial acne, I learned that it was NOT OK to speak up for or express myself, especially to authority figures like my parents. Stuffed anger eventually gave way to a rather unpleasant ulcer! My voice became suppressed as I perceived that I had to be perfect; my ideas were not good enough or worth sharing; and I did not believe that I was valuable enough!

A dark silence fell on my incomplete relationship with Mom on a sunny August day in 1976, as she departed without any good-byes. A cerebral aneurysm at age 40 began Mom's journey Home; mine became what I call my "dark night of the soul" —abandonment, emptiness, fear, anger, anxiety, premature adult responsibility, dreams shattered, grief, loss and special occasions without Mom's physical presence. It was a very difficult path, but one I was meant to walk. My voice appeared silent for awhile as I was constantly looking for a "mother" figure to help me find my way in life. It was a very confusing time; I was still shocked by what happened and not yet sure of my footing in the adult world waiting for me. I would eventually realize, however, that this life-changing event was the impetus for the changes that would create the life I wanted and deserved! It caused me to begin a journey deep within to the ultimate Truth of my purpose. It put me on a path to clarity where the answers lay to the many questions I had of life! Something inside me began to stir. I felt like I was just beginning to wake up after a long, long sleep!

In the late 80's, I found myself returning to school as an adult student in a Social Work program with thoughts of "saving the world!" The experience, however, saved ME as I slowly began taking a look at the thoughts and emotions that had ruled much of my life: fear, criticism, perfectionism, limitation, unexpressed anger, and low self-esteem.

My voice gathered strength throughout those three years, culminating with the Salutatory Address I delivered with grace and confidence. I will always remember the surge of energy within as I quoted one of my mentors, Oprah, that "we are born for greatness!"

Ever since that declaration, I have been gradually living into my purpose. This required a more in-depth inquiry: Who am I? Why am I here? Once I had the courage to start asking the questions, the answers began to reveal themselves, in one form or another. For the next few years, I kept walking through windows and doors of new opportunities, not knowing exactly where they were leading, yet somehow trusting the process. I gained new skills; met new people with new ideas.

As I was reinventing myself, life inside the cocoon was very unsettling, to say the least! Light began to seep through the cracks and focus on the belief systems that didn't seem to be working for me anymore. There were times when it felt awfully tight inside that cocoon, as I adjusted to new possibilities! I realized I was growing.

And continue to grow I did when I met my perfect life teacher, my husband Gary. Gradually I learned that he had his own lessons to learn as he faced many physical, emotional, mental and spiritual challenges. The years that followed also included helping my Dad and mother-in-law make their transitions in Spring, 2002. It appeared to me at times that I might not make my way out of the cocoon. The Light dimmed off and on for awhile, but when I finally decided to . . ."Close my eyes and SEE!" . . . life became much brighter. My lesson was to see these stressors as opportunities for my personal growth and transformation. There was always a Higher Plan! I chose to take better care of myself physically by walking and eating healthier. Mentally I used positive affirmations and self-talk to replace the old beliefs, and emotionally I released years of stuffed anger using mirror and Inner Child work. I even trained as a Heal Your Life workshop leader so I could teach these life changing skills to others! I learned to speak up for myself, and love for myself and Gary grew. On the spiritual front, I was led to a supportive, like-minded spiritual community where I directly experienced "Be Still and Know!" Life was now working FOR me!

Something very different was happening in the cocoon. The fuzziness of my long body was disappearing; it began to feel much lighter. I was transforming! Meditating, reading, attending classes; speaking and teaching that which I most needed to learn, I found that my purpose was indeed finding ME!

There was still some residue of fear until one day, on one of my usual morning walks, I had just paused to reflect near the top of a railroad overpass, when I heard a young man facetiously yell, "JUMP!" from a speeding car. After realizing it was ME he was shouting to, and after checking my pulse, I received the gift in the message. I've been "jumping" with more trust in the Universe ever since that day—my cocoon had cracked open!

In October, 2005, a hike with some new friends after a retreat in Sedona was well beyond my comfort zone. We climbed over huge tree limbs, and up and down red rocks, all the while getting farther and farther away from the car! My thoughts: *A simple hike? I don't like this! I just want to relax and take a shower!* It was extremely hot, the water supply was low and my leg was beginning to hurt. I decided to shift my thoughts, relax into the experience and enjoy! I did speak up for myself and, guided by Spirit, sat down on a small rock by the cool creek. There on a rock, as if it were waiting for me, was the most gorgeous Monarch butterfly gracefully opening and closing her wings for several minutes as I heard Her whisper, "You're ready to fly, Caren!" My eyes became moist as I gazed in near disbelief, but my heart knew it was True. Thanks, Mom!

I have found my Voice, born of the Silence and powered by the sweetness of Spirit. To bring forth that which is within me is my Gift of Expression. May you find yours so, together, we may make huge contributions to this world!

TRANSFORMATION!

Diana Ritchie, United Arab Emirates

"Using a combination of alternative therapies, I have completely recovered with no symptoms from the paralyzing disease."

Every once in a while during a person's life, an event occurs that so profoundly changes them, that it must be shared. In my case, one such event was an incredible healing *transformation*. Come join me on this fantastic journey of self-healing. My affirmation is that it will inspire you to overcome any illness or any challenge you may be facing in your life and lead to your own *transformation!*

Before we begin the journey, I ask that you close your eyes, take a few deep breaths and reflect on challenges you have faced, or are currently facing in your life. As we continue our journey, realize that no matter how difficult your challenges may seem you have the ability to overcome and heal them as I have, and as I like to say, it's time to begin "Healing the Whole Self."

Diagnosed with Multiple Sclerosis at 28 years of age, I was disabled for many years before I found that it was possible to "clear" the unwanted disease from my body. Using a combination of alternative therapies, I have completely recovered with no symptoms from the paralyzing disease. Let's go back in time and find out what created my disease in the first place.

The tragic death of my mother two weeks before my 15th birthday left me feeling very scared and lonely. I tried to turn to my father for comfort, but he was not very supportive. The next six months, I took on the task of caring for my father, my brother and my two younger sisters, assuming the role of my recently deceased mother.

I felt very angry that I was not allowed to do the things that other "normal" teenagers did. My father found another woman very quickly, and he moved in with her taking my three siblings with him, leaving me behind to cope for myself in the house where my mother had died. I felt terrified in the house all alone, scared to even go to the toilet in the middle of the night. Instead, I would urinate on the floor and then cover the puddle with my bedside mat praying it would be dry by morning.

I soon found an opportunity to train as an apprentice hairdresser. After six months my boss invited me to come live in the family's home as part of their family. My boss had a son and daughter. After about a year, the son became very jealous and possessive of me, especially if I brought other boys to the house.

One night I went out with a group of friends including my foster family's son. At the end of the evening he offered to drive me back to the house, but on the way he stopped in an isolated location and raped me! I was shocked and horrified that he could do such a thing. The molestation then continued for nearly 10 years! I threatened to tell my "foster mum" if he didn't stop, but he claimed he would just tell her that I had stolen something and I would be thrown out on the street. I was trapped in this living hell until I was 25 when I met and married my former husband. After I married, the foster family rejected me, telling me that I was now a married woman and they wanted nothing more to do with me.

Almost immediately after the marriage, in fact on my honeymoon, the man who I thought would change my life for the better became physically and mentally abusive. This added to the heartache and stress that I had already endured in my life.

I lived abroad in Germany with my former husband and worked as an air stewardess, my lifelong passion. During this period I was taken to the hospital suffering from acute double vision. Following two lumbar punctures I was diagnosed with Multiple Sclerosis.

Then the absolute worst thing occurred: I lost the air stewardess job I so dearly loved. I also lost the motivation to live and along with it went my self esteem! Over the next 10 years I spent a great deal of time in and out of hospitals, suffering from paralysis in my legs, arms and hands. I was even confined to a wheelchair for a while.

I now know that my illness was in fact a manifestation of the negative thoughts and emotions I was harboring from my life! According to the *Heal Your Body* book by Louise L. Hay, the probable causes were mental hardness, hard-heartedness, iron will, inflexibility and/ or fear.

The turning point came when I moved to Cyprus. One day I spotted an advertisement for a Reiki course and this opened me up to new and alternative methods of healing. I then did a Ken Keyes' week-long, intensive course, "Caring Rapid Healing," where I went through my whole traumatic life bit by bit, releasing all of the traumas that I had experienced during those times. I learned that all feelings that are unexpressed are stored subconsciously and will then create illness or even diseases in the body if not released.

Continuing with my healing *transformation*, I completed several other courses and alternative therapies, in particular Louise L. Hay's "Love Yourself, Heal Your Life" workshop. *None* of the symptoms has ever reappeared again! I had healed fully both emotionally and physically and was so excited by the results that I decided to travel to Birmingham, England to attend the Heal Your Life workshop leader training program so I could share this amazing work with others.

The alternative therapies so healed and *transformed* my life that I have since adapted the works using my own healing journey and experience to organize and conduct 10 week study courses and a variety of other weekend and one-day workshops and seminars. I also developed a unique 5-hour self-healing program (1 hour per week) for those who feel more comfortable in a one-to-one environment.

Committed to assisting others, I now help them to develop and use their inner powers to create what they want from life. This may include overcoming physical disorders, identifying and transforming negative beliefs, healing personal and family relationships, releasing resentments and long-held anger and using positive affirmations to manifest the things they want. These methods have even helped people lose weight and overcome addictions!

My self-healing journey has helped me overcome the traumas I suffered in my childhood and early adult life. It gave me the strength to end a 20 year abusive marriage and I now have a beautiful relationship with a wonderful man and life-partner. I am now embarking on the greatest healing journey of my life, the journey to assist others! If I can overcome Multiple Sclerosis, you can overcome any challenge in your life!

If the story of my healing journey has touched some "un-healed" part of you and you would like to learn more about the details of my life and miraculous healing *transformation,* look for my soon to be released book, *Transformation.*

Love & Healing!
Diana

LETTER TO AN INSPIRATIONAL FRIEND

Annie Miller, Australia

"Death belongs to life as birth does.
The walk is in the raising of the foot
as in the laying of it down. "
–Rabindranath Tagore

You have told me that you are not ready to die yet. I have heard you say that you had "so much work to do," and had "so many stories to get out there." I wonder if, in your determination to win the battle, you had neglected to notice the success of your "work," and indeed that the "stories" actually *were* "getting out there?" Over the last 6 years, since your life has taken on new challenges you have been radiantly positive.

The battle has not been easy and the casualty list is long. You had to give up your social work studies at college. The seemingly simple act of attending was defeated by your inability to drive a car or even to sit for very long in class. Completing assignments became impossible because your arms were often too painful to lift. Memory loss brought much confusion and even movement around the house caused pain. There were days when the inability to get to the bathroom without assistance was like a physical and psychological beating. Almost every month brought with it a decrease in energy and an increase in pain. Slowly your feeling of helplessness increased, and the loss of independence brought periods of anger and frustration. The weariness of it all gripping both mind and body.

But you have not given in. You were convinced that studying at college and moving ahead into the workplace as a social worker was the way that you were going to make a difference. You were going to win the battle and move on.

Sure, you have some down times. Days that find you so low that dark clouds move in and the tears flow. But you punctuate these with determined statements like "Oh, I'm fine, just a bit down. I'll be better tomorrow". You have long believed that your illness has been one of the wonderful things that has happened to you, and acted on the belief that people can create meaning and purpose in whatever life hands them.

"Your vision will become clear only when you look in to your heart; Who looks outside dreams, who looks inside awakens."-Carl Jung

It has been such a privilege to watch and share in your personal journey. Most normal people would not have been through such an amazing transformation, and indeed, not touched so many lives as you have with yours. Your growth and spiritual experience have influenced so many.

Look at your children. Your grace and love has filled them with lessons that will stay with them forever, and in time will be passed on to their children. An ex-husband has become perhaps closer to you now than he has ever been, and the richness of his relationship with the children and yourself has illuminated all of your lives.

Your family has been brought together in a way I see now would never have happened otherwise.

To all of your close friends, and there are many, you have been a gift in disguise. Even your medical teams over the years have been inspired by your inner strength and happiness. Our laughter in the oncology suite of the hospital surprised many! I know they will take that strength and use it to benefit themselves and many others.

The people you met in college will also take your story to the world. Anyone that has had a relationship with you has felt your positive influence, and I believe that influence will change the way they all view their lives.

My own children, sharing your presence as you stay with us, will grow with warmth and love in their hearts, always remembering the stories in bed, the sudoku puzzles, and the joy they feel when you are with us. You enrich all our lives, and bring great perspective and a deep peace to mine.

Even faced with the stark reality, we laugh together about many things. We chuckle about you passing your "use by" or "best before" date. We laugh about the "opiate" brain. You are living a life of purpose, without fear of death. Because, we learnt the hard way; *fear stops life* —it does not stop death! I have watched you over the years peeling back the layers of your life and deal, one by one, with any limiting beliefs, grappling with the truly authentic you. You courageously chose to do this as you face your life challenging diagnosis. You use your life experiences as a learning opportunity, to grow, evolve and lead a soul directed life.

So, consider, my friend. You ARE your work. You ARE achieving your life's purpose whilst on your amazing journey. You say over and over that you must write, that you must get your message out. I say it IS out there. It is *your presence* in everyone's lives that is the message, and in turn they will go on to share this with others.

"*People are like stained glass windows, they sparkle and shine when the sun is out, but when the darkness sets in, their true beauty is revealed only if there is a light within.*"

-Elisabeth Kubler-Ross

No one knows how long you have to go on your journey. Metastatic Breast Cancer is a fascinating beast. You have shared it all and in your own way will achieve immortality.

We love, honour and thank you from the depths of our hearts, where you will remain forever.

Annie

THE DAY I LEARNED THE VALUE OF A NICKEL AND GREW UP

Anne Humbach, New York

"While we were doing the dishes, I finally got the courage to ask her for the nickel."

It was September, 1932, and I was 14 years old. I was filled with excitement and anticipation. I was starting my first day of high school! Not just any HIGH, but JAMAICA HIGH; a brand new building, the epitome of all High Schools in NYC. It was a huge, U shaped, gray stone structure on a hill. As I entered this enormous place with a million corridors, rooms, and stairs, I was overwhelmed. I felt I was being swallowed up by it—that it would keep chewing on me for four years and then spit me out, ready or not!

At that time, we lived in Hollis, a section of Queens and quite countrified. There were small houses with vegetable and flower gardens. We children had a very long walk (about an hour each way) to school. We didn't mind, because as we walked along, our little band grew larger. It was fun, laughing, talking, teasing, pushing, and running. One day we heard exciting news! At the time our only mode of public transportation was a trolley car line. Well, it was going to be replaced by buses. Oh my, what anticipation! We had never ridden on a bus.

We all planned to ask our mothers for a nickel to ride home on the bus. I was filled with anxiety—how I was going to ask my mother for this nickel? Up to this time, it had not occurred to me why asking for money was verboten.

While we were doing the dishes, I finally got the courage to ask her for the nickel. I explained to her that all the other children were also asking for nickels so we could ride the bus together. Well, it seemed that she just froze with her hands in the dish basin. "Please Mama," I begged. She stood still for a long time. When she finally turned around, I was astonished to see tears of anger and frustration in her eyes. "You foolish girl," she said to me. "Do you not realize what a nickel can buy? It buys 5 rolls for your week's lunch box. It can also buy 5 apples for you." In the next few moments I learned about many things that could be bought for a nickel.

Then she said, "I cannot give you this nickel for a foolish bus ride!" All this time she was crying as if her heart would break. I just stood there staring at her and suddenly stupid, silly, me realized we were POOR. And just as suddenly, knew how much our mother loved us. Without complaint, she went to work as a cook every day, came home, and then took care of her family. By her thriftiness she made every nickel count and kept the heart and soul of our family together.

By this time, I, too, was crying. Before I knew it, I ran to her. We stood in that kitchen, laughing, hugging and crying together.

That was the day I grew up.

BECOMING SPIRITUAL

Peter Teuscher, Germany

"So as I sat on the plane waiting for take off, an elderly lady took the seat beside me and we struck up a conversation."

When I look back and remember the state of my life several years ago it is often uncomfortable to acknowledge some of the things about the man I used to be. However I intend to share this experience just the same, with the hope that my example may help others find the part of them which lies neglected and ignored deep within.

Mine is a story of struggle, a struggle with myself. I have overcome this internal battle by looking for the answers inside, allowing me to develop a philosophy which formed the foundation for new thinking habits, based on love, trust, gratitude, and faith. It broke down boundaries rather than constructing them and this allowed me to see the world in a way that was never possible before. Years of depression and self defeating behaviour are now behind me and so I would like to share how I created the new me.

My life didn't change over night but gradually with a great deal of resistance and through a sequence of events I would have previously considered to be coincidence. There was a time when I rejected anything which could not be clearly proven by science even though I had little or no interest in the sciences. Spirituality and religion were, for me, synonymous with superstition and anyone who believed in such things was living in a fantasy world in denial about their own mortality. Through all my smug cynicism and my undying curiosity about some people's apparent foolish reliance on faith, I was myself in denial of my own flawed sense of reality.

While there were many factors which contributed to my shift in paradigm, I can clearly remember one event which undoubtedly initiated a change in my thinking and in the course of my life. I was flying back from San Diego after a distressing visit with my girl friend at the time. It was an unhappy situation which I was desperately holding on to. She was very religious while I was an emphatic atheist, and this left her unsure about our future together.

So as I sat on the plane waiting for take off, an elderly lady took the seat beside me and we struck up a conversation. She told me she had been in San Diego to perform a wedding ceremony. *A minister?* I thought to myself, *What a perfect opportunity.* "It is interesting that we happen to be sitting together," I told her, "because I could really use the advice of someone like you right now. What a coincidence!" "I know," she responded with a smile, "I asked to sit beside you. I am a psychic minister." My immediate reaction was one of contempt but I listened on respectfully and my desperate need to share my feelings overcame my defensive cynicism.

She went on to tell me things about my life which no stranger could have known and even went on to reveal information about my past lives. Her advice was to leave the woman I was with and once I did so the right person would come into my life in no more than six months. We parted ways and although I resisted everything this woman had said, there was nothing in my logical fear based philosophy which could explain what had just happen.

I ignored all of the woman's advice at first but our chance meeting seemed to have set something in motion. Not only did I begin to re-examine my perceptions of the world but I also began to come into contact with information, people and new ideas that slowly began to pry open my closed mind.

Something was changing in me and perhaps for the first time in my life I was rethinking my very critical belief system and taking an honest look inside myself for answers. I began reading a great deal of books on personal development. I tried hypnosis to help with my motivation, which lead to meditation. After all this self searching I was forced to acknowledge I had been unhappy for some time. This admission lead me to finally seek therapy where I began to understand that I had been suffering from depression.

It was at a friends party that I discovered a book on past life regression. Perhaps it was the fact that another friend had just sent out an email about her experience with regression work or the words of the woman on the plane, but the book really jumped out at me. So I borrowed it and read it the next day. My appetite for more information and new ideas was growing by the day and it wasn't long before I embarked on my own life changing experience with regression therapy.

Slowly but surely I was developing a new philosophy which was based on living a happier life rather than appeasing my fears. It took a while but I began to take the advice of the psychic woman. Almost one year later I broke up with the girl in San Diego. Once I finally decided I would never go back to her, I met Michaelle, who is now my wife.

It was while I was listening to the tape of a session which Michaelle had with a psychic medium named Gloria, that I found myself compelled to have my own session, even though I have never been a fan of psychics or being told my future.

Gloria's gift is one that allows her to communicate with those unseen to most of us. During the session, as she described the person she was in contact with, she would occasionally stop abruptly to say: "All right I'll tell him." She would then go on to relay some information. Her accuracy in describing family members and situations quickly gained my confidence. Then came something completely unexpected. Gloria told me that someone who called himself Robert wanted to work with me to write a book. It would be important stuff which should be published. There was nothing of the subject matter only that I should begin by the end of that coming January.

In January the idea hit me like a hammer and I became inspired to write to the point that I would have sessions where I could barely punch the keys quickly enough. However it didn't take long for the old voice of doubt to discourage me and after only a few months the book lay dormant.

Then something incredible happened. Dr. Jonni O'Connor, someone I had worked with but to whom I hadn't mentioned Robert, passed on a message to Michaelle. The night before someone named Robert insisted she pass on a message that I must continue to write. That was enough to regain my confidence so I continued, often with long pauses but never giving up. After almost four years the book has evolved, as have I, and the first draft is finally complete.

I have learned that the answers lie within us and that Love supports us while fear inhibits us. The book has taught me and now, though it once seemed so unlikely, I am ready to teach others who are open and ready to learn.

WELCOMING CHANGE
Dawn Bradley, England

*"When I'm afraid to change something in my
life, I remember a time when I had the courage
to make a change, and it really paid off."*

Do you recall a time when you were reluctant to change something in your life? Did you ever visit the hairdresser, intent on having a wildly different style, only to come out with exactly the same style you went in with, but just half an inch shorter? Perhaps you went ahead and found the courage to have the wildly different hairstyle, and then cried all the way home because it was just TOO different?

Sometimes we let our imagination run riot, and think about all the ways where changes can go wrong. We think of the worst possible outcome and we cannot sleep or think of anything else. It becomes overwhelming. Our bodies are flooded with adrenalin, which makes us feel anxious and unsettled.

When I'm afraid to change something in my life, I remember a time when I had the courage to make a change, and it really paid off. By focusing on positive experiences, and re-living them in our mind's eye, the cells in our body are triggered to re-experience the positive outcome. This floods the body with endorphins, which makes us feel happy.

This is one of my success stories:

A few years ago I decided to take six months travelling around New Zealand. When I arrived at the hostel, I advertised for someone to share a car and the experience with me. Timna replied and so we set off on our adventure.

After ten weeks of fun had passed, Timna had to return home, so I decided to contact a couple I had met whilst travelling around Australia earlier that year. Lynn and Noel had invited me to stay with them if I ever made it to New Zealand.

Lynn met me at the airport, and I received a very warm welcome into their home. I was made to feel like a very special guest. They had prepared a beautiful bedroom for me to use during my stay, and Lynn gave me some of her clothes, knowing that I would welcome the change from my backpacking attire. It was an unexpected gift that I truly treasured.

Lynn and Noel arranged for me to meet their friends at parties and at the polo club. They even introduced me to a holistic therapist, Gill, knowing that we would have lots in common. I made good friends with Gill, and had lots of fun too. Gill also introduced me to her friend Eileen, and the three of us would meet to chat over hot chocolate. Eileen then introduced me to Ceroc…a fun way to dance, socialise and keep fit all at the same time!

Every morning Noel brought me breakfast in bed: a delicious bowl of porridge and a cup of tea. It was pure bliss after the early starts when I had been backpacking around the country. Lynn and Noel even went away for the weekend, and entrusted me with the run of their beautiful home.

After a couple of weeks, I realised that it was time for me to move on. I didn't want to overstay my welcome, and I decided to look for more permanent accommodation. I had fallen in love with Christchurch and its people, and wanted to spend a few more months there. Lynn helped me to look through the flatmate adverts in the newspaper, and told me the location of the best places in town.

Lynn and Noel went along with me to check out some of the rooms, but none of the places appealed to me. They weren't as nice as the home I was staying in and I was also worried about losing the network of friends that I had recently built up. So I decided to increase my budget. Somewhere in my head there was a little voice saying, "I'm worth the extra few dollars, and it will open up a bigger choice to look at." I acted on this and telephoned one of the adverts, arranging to meet a lady at her home. Off I set. It was a long walk and a warm day, and I arrived at the house all hot and sweaty. As I walked up the driveway I could see that this was also a very beautiful home and I started to worry that I looked bedraggled from my walk.

I rang the doorbell and was greeted by a tiny lady, petite and well groomed—my heart sank. I wished I could have made a better first impression. The lady welcomed me with a big smile and took me into the lounge. Everything looked brand new and it was so immaculately clean I was scared to sit down in case I made the place look untidy!

Lexia chatted with me about the room that she had available and she showed me round. This boosted my confidence, as obviously Lexia wasn't as worried about my appearance as I was. The room was large and bright and had its own deluxe ensuite bathroom. My heart raced with excitement at the thought of living in such a beautiful home.

Lexia then gave me a tour of the house. Everything was so stylish and chic. I had such a good feeling about Lexia and the house, and the smile on my face became bigger and brighter. I *really* wanted to live there.

The delight must have been written all over my face when Lexia asked me if I would be interested in taking the room, and I said "yes" before she could change her mind! I moved into the house the following day and was taken out for dinner by Lexia and her family. I felt so welcomed into this family.

The next day Lexia handed me a massive pile of designer clothes that she no longer wanted. She then gave me some brand new shoes that fitted me like a glove. To top it all, Lexia announced that she owned two cars, and as she could only drive one at a time, I could help myself to the keys and have unlimited use of the other car. (The other car was a brand new, sporty, red 4 x 4.) I really felt like one of the family.

I couldn't believe my luck. This was truly amazing! There I was worrying about moving forward, and all the time, this was all just waiting for me.

I stayed with Lexia for four months until I returned to England. She calls herself my second Mum, and we keep in touch via email. Zara and Eileen have been to visit me in England, and Gill is planning to come and visit next year. We all keep in touch by email and phone and I'm looking forward to seeing them all in New Zealand very soon.

I'm so glad that I listened to my inner voice and trusted in the abundance of the universe. I was certainly well rewarded with kindness, generosity and friends for life.

TRANSFORMATIONAL FENG SHUI

Barbara Andranowski, New York

*"At first, I noticed interesting shifts
taking place in my life, but then a whole
new path opened up for me."*

It's interesting how one is led to certain things. Always being a lover of the metaphysical and esoteric subjects, a friend of mine gave me a gift certificate to a New Age bookstore for my birthday. I had decided to pick up a few things when a Feng Shui book on the shelf caught my eye. I was familiar with the subject but knew little about it at the time. The girl working at the store started to tell me all the benefits she received as a result of practicing Feng Shui. You may be thinking, what is Feng Shui?

Originating in China, Feng Shui means wind and water, and is also known as the art of placement. It is being in harmony with your environment and creating a healthy flow of energy in your space. There are different schools of Feng Shui, but the one I studied and practice is the Black Hat style. In this style, we work with the Bagua, an 8-sided, octagon- shaped map. Each area of the Bagua corresponds to a different life area.

The life areas are: Prosperity, Fame/Reputation, Love/ Relationship/Marriage, Creativity/Children, Helpful People/Travel, Career/Life Path, Skills/Knowledge, Family/New Beginnings, and Health (Center).

Back to the bookstore: the Feng Shui book spoke to me, so I decided to take it. Reading it, I became fascinated with the subject. Having an Art and Design background, I felt it was right up my alley! Learning about all the interesting cures, I couldn't wait to put all the suggestions into action!

I went down to Chinatown in New York City and picked up many of the suggested items and objects to use for successful cures in the life areas. I felt I Feng Shui-ed my space perfectly and wanted to see what would happen! But some time passed, and I was growing impatient. I thought to myself, *Did I do this right? Is this working?* At the time, I was unaware that I was on the brink of change.

I learned about a training program here in New York to become a Feng Shui Consultant and decided to sign up for it! I was excited and felt that by being in the training program, I would really get the true understanding on the subject and really know how to put it all into action correctly.

As it turned out, the Feng Shui program I signed up for wasn't exactly all about color, design, or re-arranging furniture. It was much deeper than that. It was about connecting to the inner self and making inner changes in order to reflect those changes in your outer world. And I was willing to go deep within myself on the inner journey.

In the program, we had a monthly buddy to pair up with and visit each other's spaces. During the visit, we would exchange suggestions, insights and feedback on each other's space. I remember one visit in particular. Early in the course, one of my buddies came to my "perfectly Feng Shui-ed" space (or so I thought) at the time. She took a look at my space and asked me the significance of some of the objects I used as cures and what they meant to me. I looked at her puzzled at first and then admitted that I read in one Feng Shui book that these were 'good cures' to use. She replied that they may be good cures, but if they don't resonate with me, they may not be the best items to use. She suggested that I change the items to things that hold more of a personal meaning to me.

So back to the drawing board I went. I reflected on what made me feel prosperous, romantic, successful and so forth and then surrounded myself with items that reflected that back to me so I would feel the vibration of it every time I looked at it.

I discovered the work of a number of spiritual teachers along the way whose work really spoke to me, especially Louise L Hay. Her work focuses on self-love and acceptance, uncovering limiting beliefs and working with affirmations. It was so valuable for me that some time later, I decided to do the Heal Your Life, Achieve Your Dreams training program to immerse myself deeper into the process and to learn how to share this work with others.

This work complemented the Feng Shui program wonderfully and I decided to blend in Louise's philosophy with the Feng Shui. I believe the process of unraveling limiting beliefs is very important because outer changes can occur instantly in Feng Shui, but the inner shifts are what make the lasting results.

It all started coming together and I felt a new me emerging: transformation was taking place! I realized the significance of clearing out the old and making room for the new, figuratively and literally! And more importantly, what you wish to experience on the outside must first be created in your heart, on the inside. Visualizing and affirming it and fueling it with the feeling create the reality you want! It was quite a transformational time for me. I felt it was something that had such significance for me that I wanted to share it with others. I worked in this method with numerous people and clients in consultations and found it to be very successful. Blending in the artistic and decorative touches is the icing on the cake! Now I see Life as an ongoing journey. There is always more to learn and discover along the way. But more importantly, I've learned to have faith in my dreams, goals and desires and believe they're already happening and on the way!

A Slice of Time

Caroline Manning, England

*"In the quiet and calm of the summer
afternoon I found myself smiling…and
smiling because I was smiling."*

The morning was busy and frantic, running round tidying rooms, picking up socks, making calls, wiping noses— the "to do" list went on and on. I had just finished loading the washing machine when my tummy rumbled and reminded me it was time for lunch. Glancing at the clock I gasped. It was 11:45a.m., the morning had flown by and I had not stopped for a single minute!

There has to be a space for me in the day, I thought as I prepared sandwiches. I felt quite alarmed. Having a space to look forward to was the thing that kept me sane. I took a long, calming breath and decided I would carve out some time for me as soon as I put the girls down for their nap, which would be perfect.

I cleared lunch time cups and plates away then washed fingers and faces and when that was all done I took baby and toddler upstairs. I tucked each child into bed and watched their soft curling eyelashes slowly close as the need for sleep took over. The aroma of warm babies made my heart swell with love and wonder. They settled quickly and when they began to snore softly, as only babies do, I realised for the first time how tired I was too. *I could happily sleep now,* I thought wistfully, but I wanted my time out in the sunshine more.

Carrying the baby monitor, my journal and a cold drink, I made my way out to the garden. Settling into a wide based wooden chair I felt supported and strong. After writing briefly of the tasks already done and the remaining tasks "to do," I put my journal aside.

It truly was a glorious day. I had found my calm oasis in the middle of a storm. As I sipped the sparkling lemonade my gaze wandered, soaking up surrounding colours: vivid pink pansies, luscious green ferns, deep red brick work, and crisp clean window frames.

The sun rose high in the summer sky, a sky clear and blue as far as the eye could see, interrupted only by occasional aeroplane trails. I could hear birds cheeping overhead, the fizzy "pop" of lemonade bubbles and the distant buzz of insects. I sighed deeply and felt myself sink into a quiet space in my mind.

For the first time that day I stopped being busy; stopped thinking, talking, rushing, doing; finally, I was still.

In the quiet and calm of the summer afternoon I found myself smiling…and smiling because I was smiling. Sitting still, removed from my daily tasks and roles, I felt grateful for this space and very blessed to have this chance to simply be. I was satisfied—completely at peace with myself and my world.

As if on cue a small and incredibly beautiful blue butterfly chose to glide over the fence into the airspace of my garden. This butterfly was flying around as though on a blustery breeze, rising and dropping, erratic and new.

I wondered if he had just a moment ago completed his transformation from caterpillar to butterfly. I watched, and was captured by the beauty of this little butterfly, experimenting with his wings, his determination, his new found flight. He landed lightly on the freshly cut grass just a short distance away from me and stood still, barely moving his wings.

He took off again and I noticed that each time the little butterfly lifted into the air, his flight was subtly smoother, subtly stronger. He was visibly growing in strength and confidence. I was full of admiration and entirely mesmerised.

The butterfly rose again, high in the air, almost over my head and I caught my breath as he gently fluttered down towards me. He landed. I felt his miniscule feet tickle my leg. He was so close that I could see in detail the magnificent sheen of blue and the starkly contrasting black markings of his wings. Wings made with the intricacy and fine detail of lace work, the petite bowed antenna and his curly drinking straw. He was beautiful, tiny, and on my leg!

Little butterfly was very calm and I was absolutely thrilled. "Hello beautiful butterfly," I spoke softly as I realized I'd been given a very precious gift.

The sun was warm and little butterfly started to groom his body while gently sunning his wings. He was so delicate and fragile yet strong and flexible. As I sat with him a profound sense of peace and joy washed over me.

Moments passed by in quiet, timeless observation. Then somehow I became aware that the moment felt complete, as if it had drawn to a natural end. As the thought appeared in my mind, the butterfly flexed his wings and departed as though he too felt the end of our time together had come. I heard myself say, "Thank you little butterfly," as he fluttered over the fence and out of my sight. He was stronger and more capable than when he had first entered my garden only a short time ago. "Wasn't that totally amazing!" I said out loud, to no one in particular.... Suddenly, I became aware of the sound of distant cars. The baby monitor crackled into life as the children stirred from their afternoon nap, perfectly timed. Rising from the garden chair, I felt newly energised and found myself reflecting on how very precious my gift of time this afternoon had been.

From that day to this I continue to create a slice of time to be still each day. Whether I enjoy my time indoors or outdoors I always smile when I remember the joy of meeting my little blue butterfly.

THREE GOLDEN KEYS

Val McCrae, Australia

*"And magically, our bodies and lives
respond in the best possible ways."*

Many years of working as a counsellor, trainer and life coach, coupled with a passion for my own and other's personal development, have led me to the conclusion that there are three golden keys to keeping life on a positive path. When used, these keys open the heart to love and acceptance of self and others, the mind to learning, and doors to new opportunities and wonderful life experiences.

How well I remember the very first self-help book I ever read, *Your Erroneous Zones* by Dr. Wayne Dyer. At the time of reading, I was in my late twenties and in the middle of a caravan holiday with my husband and two young children. Wow… this stuff was an eye-opener to me. What I mainly got from it was the earth-shattering message that I was responsible for my own life. How could this be? Parents, school and women's magazines had promised my generation of women that a man would come along and make us happy. This was the deal I had anticipated. I was not particularly happy at the time, and I was still waiting for my husband to put this right for me. The idea that I was completely and utterly responsible for my own happiness *and* my own misery was a new one and not one that I was willing to take on board immediately. But gradually I accepted the first key: I am responsible for my own life.

And so it was that through the following years, while embarking on my own formal training to be a teacher and counsellor, I began a lifetime's focus on my own mental, emotional and spiritual development. This concept of self-responsibility became real and of great significance in my own life and in my work with others. Nowadays, it is not that unusual in my life-coaching practice to spend the best part of many sessions helping a client to "get" this for themselves. So often, clients will tell me that they would be happy except that someone else, a significant other, a parent, a child, colleague, sibling or friend, is somehow blocking their progress. Hopefully, the process of understanding and self-responsibility may begin. Once established, wonderful transformation can take place.

In reality, each one of us is responsible for our choices, our decisions and our behaviour. If this understanding begins to expand from the merely psychological to encompass the spiritual as well, a new and exciting path may be walked and a life-long journey begun. We can now own the first golden key.

And the second key? Well, if you and I are going to accept responsibility for our own lives in every way, we had better make sure we love ourselves enough to trust that we will do a good job. My second key is to love and accept myself just the way I am. This is the primary message of Louise Hay and many other authors. Louise explains that no matter what issues her client may present, she always works with helping them to love themselves more. When I read this again after many years of having it at the back of my mind, I had one of those wonderful "aha" moments. Yes, this is the common factor when working with people, even from diverse backgrounds with a variety of life issues. This is the core to progress and change.

How many years did I struggle, feeling "not good enough," inadequate and unworthy of the best things in life? Too many, I fear. Even more tragically, as a young mother in my twenties, I was not able to teach my children to love and accept themselves either. While I wish I could do it all again, all I can do now is share what I've learned.

Realising that we all have our shadow side, our demons and weaknesses, can we love ourselves anyway? We struggle so much with this concept, saying that this is self indulgent, arrogant and selfish. But, this is not the kind of love we mean. Rather it is loving ourselves as spiritual beings. It is the love and compassion we might give to a small child or our best friend. What we need is this non-judgemental love to encompass our many struggles, the forgiveness for all our mistakes, as well as the appreciation of our achievements and efforts. It is a truism that if we cannot love and accept ourselves we will never really love, accept, and be totally 'there' for others. When we accept, rather than resist and battle with, our negative thoughts or our annoying habits, it becomes more likely that we can change them.

Loving ourselves is not such a complicated matter, so let's not leave it until tomorrow or next week, let's start today and right now. Imagine this love then spreading to your neighbours, your family, your friends, and anyone you meet. If we are all busy spreading love and compassion it will become a worldwide movement. What could be more important than this second key?

And last, but not least on this very special key ring is the key that allows us to create our own reality: the power of our minds. So many inspiring authors have written about this concept in one form or another including: Louise Hay, Wayne Dyer, Deepak Chopra, and Shakti Gawain to name but a few. This seemingly mysterious idea has been the hardest of all for me to come to terms with. I have resisted the idea over and over again while simultaneously battling with its magical possibilities. What does it mean then? Let's simplify.

Well, having taken a comfortable grip on the first two keys so that in a state of self-love we are taking responsibility for our decisions and choices, we begin to realise that we can control our thoughts. Thoughts constantly enter our minds—no matter what we may be doing. But they are only thoughts, and thoughts can be changed. HOW? Well, once we realise we are thinking thoughts of anger, jealousy, self-pity, lack, fear and other negative and self-destructive ones, we can consciously re-frame these. There is always another way of viewing a situation. But then, we go further. We can begin to create more and more positive thoughts and ideas to fill our days and our lives. We call these affirmations. They are positive statements such as, "My life is filled with an abundance of love and joy." Or more specific ones like, "At this meeting, I will exude love to all and love will come back to me." There is an infinite variety of these statements to cover every thought and situation in our lives. We may say them, sing them, write them or meditate on them.

Additionally, we can use the wonderful technique of visualisation. There is nothing particularly weird or difficult about this. Instead of letting ourselves imagine an assortment of possibly negative and unpleasant scenarios, we consciously create peaceful, successful, and joyful pictures of wonderful outcomes for all situations.

And suddenly, this large and limitless space of unending potential that we call our 'mind' is working for us rather than against us. And magically, our bodies and lives respond in the best possible ways.

Please share with me the incredible 'unlocking' power of these special keys and trust them to work for you to improve your life. When we learn to unlock the mystery to our own lives, we may get copies of the keys cut and give them to others so that eventually, the whole world may become more open to ideas of happiness and generosity.

THE GIFT

Y'vonne Cutright, Oregon

". . . I would hear a tiny voice from
someplace near my heart say, 'You will make
it through this; you will be all right.'"

Many years before he died, John's feedback to me was: "You will always do all right no matter what happens in your life." I'd almost forgotten it until I read something about feedback being a gift.

My husband was a very successful business man who enjoyed being able to provide a wonderful life for all of us. Our four children all attended private schools, and we had a very large, well-lived-in home. I traveled to many countries with him, with my children, with friends, and even alone on occasion. I had the pleasure of being the recipient of his generosity in many ways and on many occasions. Just a few examples: a birthday gift of tickets to England for my sister and me, a wonderful new sports car in the driveway upon returning from a trip, and a ski trip to Austria with a friend because there was no local snow. I will forever be grateful for having lived such a wonderful life with him for so many years.

I never thought about those words of his during our life together, why would I? Everything would always be fine, what could change? Only everything! I knew shortly before John died our financial situation had changed; I had no idea just how much!

My life changed forever that cold, rainy February morning my husband died. What I remember most about those days in intensive care with him was the rain hitting the windows and watching it stream downward, making paths that led nowhere; where did it go after hitting the bottom of the window? I remember thinking the same thing immediately after he died: *Where did he go? Where did his spirit go?* That was no longer the person I knew lying in that bed. Where did he go?

How does a person walk out of a hospital alone, without the person she had shared 35 years with not being by her side? We went in together, we should have left together; it didn't happen that way. That life was over.

I remember very little of the next few weeks other than I felt as alone as anyone could ever feel. I don't remember conversations with my children, who were feeling as much pain as I was; I have no idea what we talked about, what I did, or what they did. I never realized that grief could be so encompassing or disabling.

A month after John died, my mother moved to Portland to be closer to me. We soon learned she had cancer, something she didn't know until she became ill shortly after arriving. I cared for her the next nine months until her death. I lost two of the most important people in my life within nine months of each other—that is hard!

Once I discovered the true state of my finances, I knew I would have to support myself, something I hadn't done since I quit teaching years ago, after our first son was born. If it was to be, it was up to me.

"I am confident, capable, and determined; I can do anything. I am in charge of my life." This became my mantra. But it seemed like a lie. How can a person be confident, capable and determined when she isn't fully functioning on any level? I have no idea how many times a day I spoke those words over the next two years. Most of the time I had tears falling down my face as I repeated them. It might have been funny if the circumstances were not so serious.

As I was repeating my mantra, now and then I would hear a tiny voice from someplace near my heart say, *You will make it through this; you will be all right.* I'm not sure where it came from but I started listening for it to see if I could hear it more often.

I had no self-confidence, no belief in myself and couldn't see how I would ever be "all right" again, whatever that meant. I also had no one to talk to other than my sister in Arizona; she was my savior in so many ways.

Gradually I started believing my mantra of being "confident, capable and determined." I realized I had to change my thoughts, attitude and feelings toward life and my job as a realtor. I had to make some hard decisions. It was a necessary step as part of the growth process I was experiencing, and I was growing and becoming stronger every day.

Finally, I realized I *would* be "all right." With wonder and excitement, I thought abut the life I could create for myself. Life as I had known it before was never to be again; I had an opportunity to create a second life for myself and that is what I am still doing.

I have changed in so many ways, learned so much about who I am and experienced personal success on a level I never thought possible. My wish for everyone who experiences loss of a loved one is that they are able, at some time, to recognize the strengths they developed through their relationship with that person, be grateful for the times they shared together, honor those times and grow into their own greatness as a result of having known, loved and been loved by that person during their lifetime together, however long or short that was. I could not have done these things without the strong support of my children, family and friends – they were all strength for me.

The only person we share a lifetime with is ourselves; we owe it to ourselves to grow and develop to be the greatest we can be for the betterment of ourselves and our remaining family. I know John would be pleased to know I have "done all right" even though my world, as I knew it with him for so long, changed that day he died; his feedback was truly a gift to me. I just wish I could hear him say, "See, I told you so!" and perhaps on some level, I have. Thanks John, for the gift!

THE VALLEY OF THE ANGELS
Angeliki Gael Kohilakis-Davis, New York

*This story is dedicated to my brother, George
Kohilakis, who unexpectedly passed on
to the next world at only age forty-eight
while sleeping on January 5, 2006.*

On the first Sunday in November, 2002, my
brother George called and asked, "Can
you be ready to leave for Greece in two
days?" By Wednesday afternoon of the same week, we
were both on a plane. Destination: Athens. A commuter
flight to the island of Crete would complete the first
half of the round trip fare. Purpose: to harvest the olives
from the eight hundred trees that were growing on our
family's farm within a time span of a week and a half.
We were "Gringos." All we knew was that most of the
olives would be cold-pressed to make olive oil and that
the Kalamatas were to be hand-picked and cured in a
vinegar brine for one month before they were deemed
to be edible. We were embarking upon an adventure
that would prove to be almost impossible.

This would be our first experience with harvesting
olives. Our father, John Kohilakis, was not well enough
to fly and no one was living on the farm. We both spoke

broken Greek, which further enhanced our main handicap: not enough time.

The ranch-style house had been built by my father, seven years ago, in a place that the Cretans called Akrotiri. There were originally two hundred Koroneiki olive trees planted on a little over a hectare, which is the European equivalent of two and a half acres. In the seven summers following the completion of the house, my father had managed to interplant six-hundred more. Almost one-hundred and fifty of these were Kalamata trees. The Greeks in the area said that they were not indigenous to the local terrain and that they would never bear any fruit.

This particular piece of property was part of a sloping valley which stretched north to the Mediterranean Sea. The view from the windows in the living room gave way to the mountains that marked the eastern border of numerous olive groves, where the Agia Triada monastery had been built into the dark, mountainous rock many years ago. The movie, Zorba the Greek, had been filmed near this location, in a tiny little sea-side village called Stavros.

Souda Bay was to the south, behind the high hills, flanked by the larger White Mountain range that had snow on its' highest peaks. This wondrous snow seemed to glitter with gold every morning as the sun would begin to rise, just before the dawn became alive. If you walked about fifty feet, southeast, from the house to the old stone cistern in the mid- afternoon, and turned to face north, you could catch a glimpse of the sunlight sparkling as if it was a plethora of diamonds, dancing upon the azure sea. If you continued walking southeast to the dirt road that led up to the high hills, as twilight's lace slowly descended upon the olive groves, your eyes, sweeping westerly, would be rewarded by the sunset spilling over Souda Bay's White Mountains. Cascading pastel-colored rainbows would gracefully disappear into the Mediterranean Sea, taking your spirit to a place where it had never visited before.

From the kitchen window, which faced southwest, I could see Agia Zoni, a small royal blue and white Greek Orthodox Church, perched upon a lonely, stone-studded hill. Grapefruit, orange and lemon trees, happily bearing fruit, flanked the veranda which extended from the kitchen's sliding door. Citrus trees also lined the meandering dirt road which was used as a driveway, as well as an entrance way into the magical olive grove.

Olives, some the size of plums, had weighed down the branches of the Kalamata trees. After the trees were relieved of their burden and the olives were placed into earthen colored jugs with brine to be cured, the silvery leaves of the Kalamata trees would start to flicker back and forth once again, as their branches swayed with the course of the wind.

I brought home a small bottle of olive oil from our harvest. It is kept in a cupboard on the left side of my kitchen sink. Every now and then, I open the bottle and slowly inhale the essence of the olives. It has an after-the-rain, earthly, fruity, slightly pungent aroma. It reminds me of how George and I apprehensively waited five days for the rain to stop, so we could start our work. It reminds me of how eight Albanian refugees, who anxiously and gratefully worked for an honest day's wage, helped us bring in sixty-five thousand kilos of olives to be cold-pressed within a short span of six days. It reminds me of the herd of goats and sheep that happily devoured the small olive leaf branches that were sorted out from the grid, right before the olives took the last part of their journey on the conveyor belt to the olive press. It reminds me of the grey-bearded priest who drove up the mountain in an old blue, battered pick-up truck, to bless our oil as it filtered into a white, fifty-five gallon drum. It reminds me of how my brother and I, with olive-scented sweat dripping from our pores, became attuned to the seasonal force of energy that had also been experienced by our ancestors throughout the many centuries before. A gift of shared consciousness had been bestowed upon us.

My fondest recollections came from when the olive grove would give a deep sigh of relief, every afternoon at four o'clock. That was the time when George would drive the Albanians back into Hania, which was their home town. Devoid of human hands, the trees would reclaim their own energy and there was a peaceful hush that could be felt throughout the gentle slopes of the valley. This was my favorite time. For one hour I would be by myself and I could reflect upon the activities of what was brought forth throughout the day. Softly walking in between the trees, I would slowly make my way to the dirt road which led up to the high hills. I was enthralled with the experience of catching the multi-colored light of the sun, which shimmered across the Mediterranean Sea as it started to set, just before the blanket of nightfall descended.

On one such afternoon, a few days before I was to leave to go back home to Long Island, New York, I felt the Kalamata trees beckon to me as I started my way softly across the olive grove's floor. I stopped for a few moments to watch their silvery leaves flicker as the waning sunlight danced along with the rhythm of a visiting, gentle breeze. It was then that I realized, if I stood still long enough, I could hear the leaves whispering to each other. And if I slowly walked a few steps closer, to become embraced by their auric field, I could hear them delicately whisper to me, "This is the Valley of the Angels."

JOURNEY TO EMPOWERMENT

Bethany Elizabeth Fraser, California

*"My life is different now; I get up each day happy
in the present and looking to the future."*

It was a typical American family that I was born
into. I say typical because we were what the
consensus spoke of as the norm; we always
went to church every Sunday, never missing a week.
We went to school like other children during the
week, with a sprinkle of after school activities and
hobbies for fun. My dad, being the sole breadwinner,
worked at a full-time job. He had built up his career
to be successful enough to the point of putting us in
the upper middle class. Mom worked as a full time
housewife: cooking, cleaning, playing chauffeur and
just keeping everything together. By day we were the
typical American family, but by night when the curtains
went down and the front door closed and locked, we
weren't quite so typical anymore. There was emotional,
mental, physical, sexual, and even ritual abuse. To say
that life was a challenge would be an understatement.

The abuse began at a young age, so by the time

I started school, I had already begun to believe that I was unacceptable, not good enough, separate, and different from most kids. School helped though, because at school the secrets of home life could be buried and forgotten for a few hours a day, easing the constant fear just a little. School also gave me a chance to do some things I found I was good at. In track and field I would place first or second in most races, discovering that I love to run. The music program offered an opportunity to sing and build upon my love of music. I also noticed a strong connection with other kids who had unhappy home lives.

As the years went on I created ways of coping with the struggles of home life. Somehow, I developed a belief that all this could be overcome. Positive thinking and encouraging self-talk became two of my greatest tools.

Time passed, and I was now old enough to get out on my own. I began looking for ways to empower myself and build my self-esteem. I read self-help books, went to therapy when finances allowed, and continued talking positively to myself. I kept telling myself I could do it; I could overcome the fear, hurt, and dislike for myself that I had come to believe was a normal part of life. One of the things I found the hardest to do was to talk to people who could help me. I had become closed off to trust and communication. I didn't know who would hurt me and who would help me. It took some time and a consistent commitment to getting to know me and who I really wanted to be. Throughout it all I gained tools that helped me love and accept myself. As a result I met someone I really like: ME!

My life is different now; I get up each day happy in the present and looking to the future. I work at a job I love, teaching people the tools to empower themselves to create a life they look forward to living. I still use some of the same tools I created for myself as a child:

music, running, writing, expressing myself on paper and positive self-talk. I have added some new tools: self-improvement seminars, the beach, friends that I truly share myself with, and a spiritual connection with the universe. As I look back on my life, I see my past as a definite challenge, my present a celebrated victory, and my future with weaknesses transformed into strengths.

The greatest challenge is always only in our minds: decide to create a victory and stand tall in the strength of a joyous celebration of who you can become!

CAUSE OR EFFECT?

Kam K Dhanda, England

*"Within you lie all answers, true
greatness and unconditional love."*

When I was a child I felt life just happened
and that I had no say in it. Some experiences were good, others were uncomfortable or painful and even at times unbearable. From a
very young age I decided that the only way to cope in
life was to be nice and try to control as much as I could.
I thought if I could anticipate people's needs then I
could control their response to me and I could make
sure that they liked me. This way, I wouldn't have to
face criticism, rejection or confrontation and would
possibly avoid abuse. I decided to control my feelings
too, in that I stopped sharing them with others and
then eventually, with myself. You see as a child, when
I did share my feelings, the reaction I got back was not
to my liking. I didn't feel validated and it seemed to
me that I just upset the people around me. The adults
around me did love me, but they didn't know how to
show their love and they couldn't see what I was go-

106

ing through. I learned to keep my feelings to myself. I ignored my needs and pushed the pain deep inside. Continuing to live an unconscious life I became what other people wanted me to be, yet all along, I knew something was not right and that things were not meant to be this way.

As I got older, I began to blame others for what was going on in my life. I felt I had many problems. Dad drank heavily and I thought if I could just get him to stop drinking and get help for him, then my life would be a lot better. I thought, if I could "help" mum and the family then I would *feel* their love and approval.

It was only years later, after a disastrous short-lived marriage that I started looking at what was going on in my life. I had become extremely ill and my husband dropped me off at my parents' house with just a few pairs of pyjamas and a handbag. Not only was my marriage over, but I was left heavily in debt and I had lost my home and job due to the year-long illness. The man that I thought would love me, protect me and provide for me did not care about me at all, he had a completely different agenda for marrying me. I thought I was the worst victim ever, feeling completely betrayed and rejected. I was re-acting to everything from a place of deep pain and abuse. I cried a lot and felt that my heart was being shredded to pieces and I wanted life to be over.

While undergoing treatment in hospital, I witnessed someone else's pain, and that was the biggest turning point in my life. I was amazed to see how much my heart had opened to love and how much I cared for others. It was at that point that I knew there was much more to life than my experiences. My heart spoke to me saying, "within you lie all answers, true greatness and unconditional love." Somehow it felt like a switch within me going on and a little candle that was so close to going out, encouraged to glow once again. My heart opened to love and when I was discharged from casualty that night, I asked God questions about my life. It was from that moment that I started receiving answers and continue to do so.

The world started changing for me because I started changing. I surrendered my situation. I stopped reacting to what was going on around me. I stopped trying to control it or make it better. I had to let go and let God. I could not make my husband love me, I could not keep my job, I could not reverse the debt and I could not go back to my "home". The only thing that I had any control over in fact was me. I took 100% responsibility for my life and decided that life was not about what was happening to me, it was *about how I handled it...and what learning I could take from it.* I learned that the experiences I had were not me. I was much more than that. I stopped playing the blaming game and stopped seeing myself as a victim. I stopped complaining and started focussing on the solution instead of looking at and sinking into the problem. This is what is meant by living at "cause". We start seeing the bigger picture and we start seeing how life is teaching us to remember and connect to our true essence and to God and to respond to everyone, including ourselves, from a place of love, awareness and understanding.

When we live at "effect" we have all sorts of reasons and excuses to stay where we are. We complain again and again and try to convince others to see our point of view, or worse, we settle for less when we deserve so much more. Why? Because it feels safer to stay at "effect" as it's easy to blame others for what is not going "right" in our life. We want *them* to change but we could be waiting a long time and in the meantime we continue to feel treated unfairly, victimised and totally helpless.

When we live at "cause" we focus on and seek the solution that lies within us—that's empowering! No matter what is going on around us we can change things because we can decide to change ourselves. We begin to feel able and capable, and it also means we have to make decisions and take actions that will produce the kind of results we want. It means giving up the excuses and getting out there and doing. It means facing fears, taking risks, trusting and committing 100% to the solution; we go out there and make things happen instead of things just happening to us. We become the creators of our lives.

When I decided to be at "cause" and live a conscious life, I began to see lessons my marriage had taught me. I changed so much through my illness and recovered in so many ways that I started writing a book about it. I realised that what I was seeking from others, was exactly what I needed to give myself! I focussed on paying my debt off and I did. Along the way I found my purpose in life and now I live a life that I love. It doesn't matter what is going on around me. What matters is who I choose to be in every situation, and I choose to be love and see others as love and as a gift. I choose to understand what is going on and my incredible learning journey continues. Challenging events still happen, only now I am better equipped to deal with them so I welcome them, and the things I discover along the way are powerful beyond measure. So here is a question for you my friends: Which side of the equation do you choose to live on?

WORKING WITH LIFE ITSELF

Kari-Ann Regina Lamøy, Norway

*"In the glowing brightness of the midnight
sun, my thoughts about my life situation,
my future, and my life as it had turned
out, were circulating in my head."*

In just a flash while the insight is pouring
through your body on all levels, your whole
life and everything you have ever believed in
can be changed.

For me this happened at a time in my life when I
had experienced a break up with my fiancée, and was
spiritually searching for more meaning to life. At this
point I realized that I had actually coped with being a
single mother, emotionally, practically and even financially. However, a burning desire had grown within me
to do something more with my life. I decided to let Life
itself guide me on my journey; to "let go and let God."
What a wise decision it proved to be.

The turning point came late one summer night. My
children were sound asleep, and since it was such a bright
and lovely night I went out in the garden, and sat down
beneath the huge trees that surrounded my home, just
enjoying the moment in peace with my own thoughts

and feelings. In Norway we are blessed with daylight even at night during the summer, and the midnight sun is known worldwide for its beauty.

The midnight sun was absolutely stunningly bright that night. Seagulls were screaming and fighting over some fish from a boat on the fjord. I was absolutely hypnotized by the scene. Shimmering colours from the midnight sun and the breeze that swept over the magnificent fjord painted it orange, yellow, brownish and golden, with the sun as a huge light behind the artwork of nature. The mountains framed the fjord with breathtaking colours and perfect shadows; there was such perfection in this divine picture! All my senses were alert, and nothing else in the world mattered to me right then. A feeling of peace embraced me, a special connection with myself seemed to be flowing through me. I was one with the whole picture I took in. I have been blessed with growing up near the ocean, mountains and the woods, so Nature has always provided me this kind of peace. To me the very essence of Life is resting in nature.

In the glowing brightness of the midnight sun, my thoughts about my life situation, my future, and my Life as it had turned out, were circulating in my head. A warm sensation flowed into me from the grass beneath my feet and the air surrounding me. An insight started to emanate; it was truly a spiritual moment! My heart was beating so hard in my chest, and my pulse was running wild! Like a huge wave my thoughts started to form the following sentences in my head:

This is it! I am on my own! Whatever happens next in my Life is up to me. I have to take the full responsibility for my own Life, for my day-to-day Life, and for myself."

What a revelation it was! Unable to move I just sat there, thinking it through, tasting the words, whispering them to myself. For the first time in my Life the feeling of not being alone came to me, embraced me, and made me feel whole. I would always have ME in my life! There was nobody but myself to blame if anything went wrong. I felt an inner peace and contentment with this thought, and I could feel my breath calm down and my pulse return to normal. Every cell in my body told me that nature in partnership with my Higher Self enlightened me. They urged me to act on this special message in order to move on.

Previous to this experience, I had read a book called *You Can Heal Your Life,* written by Louise Hay. Now the messages of this book all came over me. Overwhelmed with gratitude, I understood that all joy, possibilities and love in the world were mine! A higher understanding assured me that it was for keepers too! I decided to start working with the affirmations again, and to have a good "house cleaning" in my life. As the big "house cleaning" within me took place, I had another insight: *this is what working with Life itself is all about*—to live in the moment, not in the past, not in the future, but here and now. I was working with Life, and enjoying every minute of it! That was why I felt so happy, and so whole. Old limitations were gone, and my focus was now on possibilities instead of limitations. Yes, I was a single mother with four children. My finances were nothing to brag about, but I had my children, I had myself, and I had a clear thought about being on the right path in my life. I felt almost electric with happiness and joy! My tremendous appetite for Life was based on the increased awareness, and all the possibilities flowed from my new insight. I was an independent individual for the first time in my life, and I loved it!

The fact that I also LOVED myself made me blossom with joy, and dance the dance of Life. I felt more grateful for being *me* than I had ever felt before. As a result I wanted to know how I could channel all this gratitude to help other people, and found myself drawn towards courses and people who would help me on my journey. I didn't even think of involving myself with a man at that time. A few months later though, after meditation and while feeling really relaxed and about to go to bed, I sat down to write a few words in my journal. I found myself writing that I was ready to meet somebody, ready to meet a man. I then described the man I wanted to meet as carefully as possible. "OK", I thought, "where did that come from?" It surprised me that I had written the words "ready to meet a man", but I closed my journal and went to bed.

The man I had affirmed for actually entered my life almost out of the blue, and proved to be the personification of everything I had written in my journal that my Mr. Right would be! Living apart the first year after we met was an important choice, a direct effect of my new feeling of being independent. Happily married today, we both value our loving, safe, and exciting life together. My husband has great understanding for my work, and we work together as a team, but we still stand tall in our own energy side by side. Kahlil Gibran expresses this so well in his book, *The Prophet*:

> "...and stand together,
> yet not too near together.
> For the pillars of the temple stand apart,
> and the oak tree and the cypress grow not
> in each other's shadow."

More than ever I now acknowledge that my thoughts create my reality, and I know affirmations work. I live my life more in the present, and I have learned how to love myself, and how to work with Life. I know that I was spiritually guided in the celestial glow and beauty of the midnight sun that very special summer night in my garden.

All is well.

POEMS FROM THE HEART

Norman Couch (1948 – 2004), England

"It was always one of Dad's dreams to get his poems published, and it has been our pleasure to be able to achieve this on his behalf."
–Dawn, Julie & Pauline

Our Dad loved to write his feelings down in poems, and we're sure that it was his way of working through his thoughts. Dad was a novice writer, but we can really feel his soul through his poetry. Some show how much compassion he had for his fellow humans, especially those less fortunate than himself. Some reflect the pain he suffered when his heart was broken yet again. Most importantly of all, some of the poems make us laugh, and allow us to remember our Dad in the way that makes us happiest: when he was loving life.

Dad died suddenly of a heart attack. He was in Thailand at the time, so none of us had the opportunity to be with him or to say goodbye. The day before he died, he had bought a piece of land near the sea where he planned to build a house for his retirement. Dad may have died with his dreams still in the planning stages, but we also know that he died a happy man. He was with a woman he loved, and he had taken his leap of faith and finally chosen to follow his heart and his dreams.

It was always one of Dad's dreams to get his poems published, and it has been our pleasure to be able to achieve this on his behalf . . .

NO!

A rattled tin
A rattled box
Twenty pence, a pound
Anything to ease your mind
You think you've helped
But have you?
No!
You just want to make a show

Mothers crying
Babies dying
Fathers looking in despair
Twenty pence, a pound
Do you really care?
No!

You pass some change
And you feel good
But there's so much out there
Misunderstood
Do you really care?
No!

You watch TV
Current affairs
More babies dying
Who really cares?
Oh my God!

How can this be?
You cover your eyes from the TV
Do you really care?
No!

A shot rings out
A young man's dead
They say for poaching
But instead
They should look at what's ahead
No food for his family
They must be fed
Twenty pence, a pound
Is it really enough to go around?
No!

Fat cats sitting at the top
Rolls Royce, fine food, Ascot, the lot
Ripping poor folk off
"You can starve, I'm the toff"
Twenty pence, a pound
A vicious circle, round and round
Twenty pence, a pound.

HAVE A HEART

Life passes by
With tears in my eyes
I sit all alone
And I moan

No one to listen
No one to hear
Just another glass
Just another beer

Family and friends
Have all turned away
They don't give a damn
Tomorrow's another day

Deep down they love me
I know this is true
But I don't accept it
So what do I do?

No one seems to love me
Perhaps I'm getting old
I'm pushed from pillar to post
And then out in the cold

I know I'm not a young man
But I've still got a heart

OUR FIRST TIME

We stood together
Alone in the shower
Our first time

It was only minutes
But it seemed like hours

To explore your body
To kiss and caress
I wanted nothing more
And nothing less

Words can't describe it
It was fabulous

MISUNDERSTANDINGS

Your friends come first
What can I say?
I'm dismissed out of the way

I ring you because I love you
Then it hurts me. Why?

I thought that things were right
But it obviously depends upon the night

You come first, always, is what I thought
The same to me is all I ask
But then you put me in the past
So few words but very hateful

Where do I turn?
What can I do?

RESTLESS NIGHT

A restless night
A thousand things on my mind
Nothing seems to fit into place
My brain runs wild
As if it has to win a race
No easy time
No slow pace

So much to look forward to
Yet it seems so far away
Will I ever reach that day?
Or will I go and ruin it
By something that I do or say?

I pray not

THE CLOWN

Life is a circus
And I am the clown
I will make you happy
I will make you frown
I may be the main act
But you will always take centre stage

SAND

We walked along the beach
We giggled and we laughed
The sun was gone, a moonless night
We were in the dark

We strolled among the sand dunes
Intent on having fun
And very quickly, our clothes came off
We were sitting on our bums!

Passion overtook us
We just wanted to get laid
But the sand came down, thick and fast
We were finding it for days

DESTINY

We met in Turkey
At the Hotel Elite
Fate cast its spell
We were destined to meet

I looked at you
You stole my heart
I knew this was it
Right from the start

Your long black hair
Your eyes of green
I pinched myself
Is this a dream?

A crowded boat
Yet no one there
Just you and me
To gaze and stare

Stolen hours
Were all we had
And for every minute
I was glad

Our past has gone
Our future's here
No turning back
Nothing to fear

You make me laugh
You make me smile
I want this forever
Not just for a while

Promise me this
And I promise you
We'll jump hurdles together
And see it through

I do believe
In a thing called fate
And that you were meant
To be my soul mate

What more can I say
Except that
I love you
In every way

Norman Couch is the dearly missed father of Dawn, Julie
& Pauline of Slough, England.

LETTING GO: THE KEY TO FREEDOM AND HAPPINESS

Jayanthi, Utah

"To me, 'letting go' meant losing all control over my life and a fatalistic acceptance of things as they were."

As a child, I found so much security and warmth holding on to my mother's sari before going to sleep that I remember the feelings even today. It had become an embarrassment for me in front of the other kids, but the thought of letting go of this clinging for comfort and support was almost unimaginable for me. I still remember the day vividly when, with a lot of determination and self control, I decided to let go of this though it seemed to be the hardest thing to do. Looking back, I think that was probably my first attempt to let go of something that was dear to me and my first step towards freedom.

We not only hold on to things in life that give us a feeling of security, but also things that cause misery and unhappiness. We hold on to emotions such as fear, bitterness, resentment and anger, all the while knowing very well how miserable these negative emotions make us feel. Apart from this, I have come to understand that holding on to anything blocks wisdom and comes in the way of our spiritual progress and freedom.

Growing up, I saw a lot of misery and suffering outside my life. I saw people suffering due to illness, poverty, natural calamities, accidents, and deaths of near and dear ones. I didn't understand why things happened as they did. Traumatized by what I witnessed around me, I spent long nights thinking about all the suffering in this world. Out of fear for my own safety and those close to me, I somehow held on to the belief that bad things were things that happened to other people. I believed no such thing would happen to me. With this strong belief in my mind, I put an insulating wall around myself and my fear. I found security in the concept that the bitter, biting cold prevailing outside wouldn't touch me as long I held on to my comforting belief of protective warmth.

Life, however, proved otherwise. I understood that I was as much prone to the world's miseries as anyone else. I then let go of my old belief, the false façade I had put around my fear. However, this did not come from a pessimistic outlook on life. Actually it was quite the opposite. I learnt to be at peace with myself and the constantly changing world, to take things as they come, to take pleasure and pain in the same stride and remain even minded and equanimous in facing the vicissitudes of life. Often times, when circumstances change in ways that we do not like, we suffer. As we learn to let go of all the protective layers we put around ourselves and our fears, we open our minds to wisdom and our hearts to kindness and compassion. I then learnt to connect to everything around me. I also learnt that all of us have access to something within that remains unchanged in spite of the changes outside and this leads to deeper levels of freedom and happiness.

Until a few years ago, I was reacting to situations in my life in the usual manner of resisting things that I did not like. But sometimes, no matter how much I resisted and how much of effort I made in trying to change a situation, things continued to remain just the way they were. I knew very well that I had to let things go in order for any change to take place. But I just didn't know how to let go. To me, "letting go" meant losing all control over my life and a fatalistic acceptance of things as they were. I definitely did not want things to be as they were. No matter how difficult or ridiculous it seemed to let go of something that I considered important, I knew that was what I had to do. So, one day as I sat in prayer, I totally surrendered to God's will. I was willing to accept anything that this universe, God, the BIG mind, the source of all creation deemed best for me, irrespective of my own desires and will. In that instant, I felt a kind of peace which I had never experienced before in my life. It is difficult to describe the feeling in words. The happiness I had derived from the things of the world seemed small in front of what I experienced. Surprisingly, within a few months after that, I got exactly what I had been striving for, though the possibility of this happening had seemed so very remote and far fetched until then.

Most often, surrender and letting go helps us to make the right kind of effort. I understood that I needed to find the perfect balance between surrender and effort in all aspects of my life. I also understood that an important factor that determines a transformation outside is a transformation within oneself.

Meditation has made it a lot easier for me to let go of things that I am too attached to. It has helped me to accept things and people as they are. It has helped me to have this attitude of loving kindness and tolerance towards all, even towards those who act in ways that I might consider wrong. It has helped me to let go of all anger and resentment I may have for any reason towards another. Though it is not always easy, this attitude of compassion, tolerance and acceptance has brought a lot of happiness and harmony in my life.

Here is an example about letting go that shows us how easy it can be. The hunters in South Asia catch monkeys using a monkey trap. A monkey trap is funnel shaped and some food is placed on the larger end. The trap is then tied to a tree with a rope. The monkey puts his paw in to grab the food but cannot get his paw out through the narrow opening as he now cannot get his fist out along with the food through the small opening. The monkey is now trapped. All he has to do to be free is to let go of the food but the monkey just doesn't realize this because of his craving for the food.

Letting go of things that trouble us is just as easy as it would be for the monkey to let go of the food, yet sometimes it seems difficult and takes tremendous determination and courage. It requires training our minds through prayer and meditation. The practice of letting go and surrender then becomes our pathway to freedom and happiness.

It is in the hour when life seems worthless and impossible that we learn what truly matters if we know how to surrender. It is in those very moments when we let go that pain gets transmuted into real joy.

PAIN AND LAUGHTER
Gail Dimelow, Spain

*"A courageous person is merely
someone who sees very clearly what lies
ahead, and goes out to meet it."*

I have always enjoyed a good relationship with my parents; they aren't just Mum and Dad, they are my pals. We relish each other's company, and can be just as well in companionable silence as in avid discussion, the conversation moving swimmingly from one subject to another. And our mutual penchant for off-beat, zany humour, always insured that there was plenty of laughter in our house. So when my father became desperately ill, and told me quite clearly how miserable and depressed he felt, my mind recoiled from watching such a beloved person suffer. I was terrified I wouldn't be able to handle it. I knew I had to do something; I knew I had to keep myself together in order to continue being of use to him, both on an emotional and a practical level.

One evening I was pondering this, and asking myself just how I was going to keep my nerve and get through it. I sat, leaning on the kitchen table, staring at the white wall, psyching myself up, like a warrior preparing for battle. This may seem an exaggeration, but that was the way it felt to me; everything looked so grim. Then I decided that all I could do was face up to it, and take whatever came.

It was a very intense moment; I was concentrating and utterly focused. Then I felt a connection, like an energy field, a live channel, going out from my face and the top of my head, to the other world, and vice versa. It seemed as though there were thin needles of life force passing through my face and head. And this brought me to clarity. I felt the darkness lift, my inner turmoil was calmed and I knew that, whatever happened, I would be alright. I was feeling all this at an emotional level, not an intellectual one, and at the time I could not put my impressions into words. But not long after I was watching a movie where a character expressed my feeling with these words: "A courageous person is merely someone who sees very clearly what lies ahead, and goes out to meet it."

And so it was; when the time came to say goodbye to my lovely Dad, I was able to do so with a light heart, knowing that I had done everything possible for him, and more.

Not long afterwards I signed up for an Aromatherapy course. You know what it's like on the first day of class: you sit down, the tutor hands out the manual and you open it immediately and leaf through, impatient to see what's inside.

The page stopped at a diagram, and for several moments I just looked at it, open-mouthed in amazement. It was an illustration, in profile, of the human head, showing lines fanning out from the eye area and the top of the head. At that time I knew very little about chakras, and there I was, looking at the sixth and seventh chakras, represented just as I'd experienced them. I closed my eyes then opened them again and looked at the diagram once more—I hadn't imagined it! I felt a surge of joy bubble up from deep within me, and glanced at the other people in the room, surprised they didn't sense my exhilaration.

First I began to smile, then to chuckle, and finally to laugh out loud! This brought a few puzzled looks from my fellow students, so I did my best to put on a straight face. But I continued to grin and giggle throughout the morning; I felt so good, I was on the right track, I wasn't alone. The Universe really did support me!

THE LEAP OF FAITH
Eva-Maria Riegler, England

"But when we focus on our goals.....that's when we can leave fears behind and do amazing things."

I t is an unusual custom they have in St. Marylebone School for Girls in London. Every morning, the girls from the whole school listen to the "Thought for the week" read to them over the Tannoy, a marvellous communication system with loudspeakers in every classroom. Each week there is a different theme. Recently it was "Confronting our fears." Four 12 year old girls in their first year have written and read out alternately to the whole school the following contribution which can be applied to any kind of fear you could encounter. Let's listen in...

CONFRONTING OUR FEARS
By Katharine Thomas, Macy Nyman, Maeve Campbell and Sarah Smith
On a school trip every student was asked to climb up a 13 meter high wooden pole, roughly the height of their school building, to get on to a tiny, wobbly plat-

form from where they had to leap through midair at a little trapeze. They then let go of that trapeze, just like in the circus, while they were lowered back down to the ground again.

Looking up at the frightfully high pole Maeve exclaimed: "Oh my goodness! There is NO WAY I am climbing up there! Leap of Faith? Leap of DEATH more like!"

Macy replied, (trying to encourage her): "You cannot possibly sit there and watch while the others are all having a go at this exciting activity."

But Maeve insisted: "I will NEVER, EVER climb up this huge shaky pole, so far from the ground. I hate heights! Even the THOUGHT of jumping into the air with nothing to hold on to is petrifying!"

Sarah chimed in with more encouragement: "All of us have been faced with fears we thought we could not overcome. A fear of heights, a fear that we don't have the right answer in class, a fear we are not cool enough, that we are not as good as those around us, not clever enough or that we don't fit in. We can feel like we've failed even before we've started. We can even feel angry when we are scared, and lash out at others, at our friends or family or teachers."

"So what can help us to overcome this fear?" asked Macy. "What is it that made Maeve and most of our friends take that *Leap of Faith* and succeed? Well, as the name of the activity suggests - it was faith. We knew we weren't really jumping out into the abyss on our own. We had faith in the safety harness to hold us and to stop us falling, we had faith in our experienced instructors to protect us and guide us, and we had faith in all our friends below cheering and waving and supporting us. All these things gave us what was needed most —faith in ourselves!

Sarah: "In the New Testament there is a story of how Peter, one of Jesus' closest friends and followers, discovered the power of faith and trust when he went out fishing with some friends one night. The waves were crushing against the boat. Suddenly they saw somebody walking towards them on the water. They were terrified.

"It's a ghost," they said, and cried out in fear. But Jesus immediately said to them: *"Take courage it is I. Don't be afraid."*

Peter replied: *"Lord, if it's you, tell me to come to you on the water."*

"Come," said Jesus. Then Peter got down out of the boat, walked on the water and came towards Jesus. But when he saw the wind, he was afraid and, beginning to sink, cried out: *"Lord save me!"* Immediately Jesus reached out his hand and caught him. *"You of little faith,"* he said, *"why did you doubt?"* (Matthew, 14:26,27)

Katharine said: "When Peter looked down and saw the waves, or looked at the wind, instead of keeping his eyes fixed ahead on his friend Jesus, that's when he began to sink.

And the same applies to us, when we focus on the problems, on the obstacles, on the fears, on our weaknesses, that's when *we* sink too. But when we focus on our goals, on our desires, on the ones around us who will support us, on the talents we have been given and on our faith in God's love for us, that's when we can leave fears behind and do amazing things. So don't look down today, look up! It is our faith in each other and in God within us that allows us to conquer any of our fears."

"The truth is: If you knew that you could handle everything that came your way - what would you possibly have to fear? The answer is: nothing!" – Susan Jeffers

Edited by Eva-Maria Riegler.

Many thanks to Hannah for bringing home these inspiring *Thoughts of the Week* and to Katharine, Macy, Maeve and Sarah for sharing them.

MAGICAL MOMENTS WITH MAYA

Susmita Barua, Kentucky

*"She gave me her usual bear hug
with a radiant smile."*

Before having my child Maya, I thought I would be the one guiding her and teaching her. Little did I know how much she would teach me, reminding me to be spontaneous, playful, and appreciative of every day life. I'd like to share with you some of my magical moments with Maya.

Newborns sleep blissfully or so we thought. That view was shattered as soon as our first-born arrived home. Maya cried fiercely as if someone just beat her blue. We rushed her to the nearest ER only to be sent back home after a long agonizing wait. Doctors had no answer for her colic. As helpless new parents we had to learn quickly how to calmly stay detached yet loving to our very distressed child. The long three-month colic ordeal left us as unpredictably as it came! This phase taught us to be more accepting of the many challenges of raising a strong-willed first child.

As soon as she could respond Maya longed for human interaction. She had no fear of adults and would often make newly-wed graduate students turn pink with her inquiry, "Where is your baby?" One day I found her pulling a visiting Professor's hand, pleading with him to come and play with her. "I am a little too old to play with you." Our senior guest kept resisting and Maya kept coaxing, "That's OK, that's OK!" At that time I was without any friends in a foreign land. I thought, if only we grown-ups could be like her!

Once my husband and I were going on a camping trip with some students and we took the back seats out of our minivan to make room for everyone. Maya was thrilled to be the center-stage with her big buddies all around her. Soon she started a game of scaring the big boys asking them "OK! Who is next? Who should I jump on now?" Her spontaneous frolics brought much laughter even to our testy friends. Her exuberant spirit would demolish all the defenses of adults.

On her third birthday I took her to the big park, but could spot no other children around. Feeling very let down from the driver's seat I asked, "Do you see anyone Maya?" She paused for a moment and said "Yes, mama!" I asked excitedly, "Where? Where?" She pointed, "Right here, you and me!" I was feeling quite lonesome at times raising an active child without any family around. Her remark made me recognize that we do have each other after all. Then I glanced around the deserted pool and said, "We need to go home, sweetie!" She exclaimed, "Look, maybe they are hiding under the water!" Her quick wit illuminated my limited mind. It made me wonder, why couldn't I even imagine that? Simply watching her play by herself made me feel whole.

While flipping through our wedding pictures in the family album Maya would often ask, "Where is me? Where is me?" I had no easy way to answer that. One day with her big imploring eyes she persisted, "Where is me, mommy?" I intuitively picked her up and went to the porch. Pointing at the moon and stars I said, "There you were!" She beamed a knowing smile that seemed to say, "Mommy knows!" Often she would ask, "Mommy did you *really* wanted a girl?" I said, "Yes, of course! How did you know?" And she would say, "*Just like me?*" I comforted her, "Yes, exactly like you, honey!" That satisfied her completely. I still wonder if she, by any means, knew my secret thoughts? It made me recall my own early childhood feeling that I somehow existed before this life began.

While shopping, I would often lose sight of Maya as she would disappear in the isles. I cautioned her not to talk to or follow any stranger in the store. She kept asking me, "Mommy, who is a stranger?" I kept quiet, as I did not want to plant unneeded fear in a friendly child. One day while strolling in the neighborhood sidewalk, we passed a new neighbor who smiled at us. Suddenly Maya yelled, "Mommy, is that a stranger?" As I tried to "hush" her mouth the right answer poured out of me. "Sweetie, a stranger is anyone who makes you feel uneasy and scared." This not only pleased her, it brought me in touch with my own feeling and how we can all use that inner sense to guide us in life.

One Sunday afternoon, as I was busy cleaning, Maya was hunting for hidden treats. She climbed up a stool almost silently to get on top of the washing machine to reach for a hidden cookie jar on the corner shelf. Her uncanny ability to locate hidden treats made me wonder whether she had some kind of telepathic sense. My own sixth sense forewarned me of her daring attempt to reach the hidden cookie jar. As I was about to scold her from behind, she plunged her hand into the cookie jar. She instantly turned back and offered me the first cookie. Her face beamed a smile of success and her gesture was one of truce. And there was a frozen moment where our fearful expectations switched and we became One! She wasn't afraid of being caught red-handed and I wasn't afraid of her falling off the stool anymore. We had a delicious moment together over a freed cookie.

Once we waited at the local airport to pick up Maya's dad returning from a business trip. While waiting, we watched the glowing red Sun gently fall below the horizon. I exclaimed sadly, "Well Mr. Sun has done his job and gone home now." "No, mommy", she said gleefully, "Mr. Sun goes home to Mrs. Sun for dinner!" Her remark transported me from feeling alienated in this mundane world to feeling connected in her magical world.

Maya picked up the habit of shouting, probably from someone in her pre-school. One day, to my shame, she started screaming loudly inside K-Mart. My instinct told me she was testing the limit of her vocal cords. I quickly took her out of the store, as she showed no sign of quitting soon. I even pressed her to keep going higher, and by her 4th or 5th attempt her voice suddenly cracked. It took almost three days for her normal voice to return. I have learned somehow that at times I must allow my stubborn child to teach herself a valuable lesson.

One fateful morning my office phone rang. To my dismay my husband informed me Maya was denied entry to her first day in school! Right then and there the ground shifted and I felt doomed for life as a mother. I was angry with the whole world for conspiring against the child and mother's great anticipation. I faxed an angry letter to the principal for failing to remind us about the required immunization paper during orientation. Coming home feeling like a loser I greeted Maya with a teary hug. She gave me her usual bear hug with a radiant smile. I told her how sorry I was that she missed her first day at school. With a carefree grin, she said merrily, "That's, OK mom. I can go tomorrow!" Her spirited presence hit me like a *Satori*. Each day is a fresh new day. To feel truly alive, we need to let go and be fully present in this moment.

MONSTERS AND BLACK TAILS

Barbara Avril Burgess, England

*"These monsters were everywhere—whenever
I went outside one would appear."*

O ne hot sunny day, when I was five, I had
been shopping with mother. We were almost home and then I could have a cool
drink of water. I turned the corner. The house was in
sight. Suddenly a big black monster appeared beside
me. I screamed and began running for home, the black
monster following me.

"Stand still." Mother shouted from the top of the
road.

I stood still, hands in the air crying and screaming.
The black monster circled me, its hot breath on my
face and legs. It sniffed every part of me. Threateningly
its orange eyes stared into mine; daring me to move so
that it could chase me again.

Mother was at my side and the black monster loped
off. "Walk slowly and it won't hurt you."

I walked as slowly as my wobbling legs and pounding
heart would allow. Once inside the house and behind

the closed door I felt a little safer but still shaky. These monsters were everywhere—whenever I went outside one would appear.

Some time later, whilst playing with friends in a small hideout we'd set up in a field opposite our home, another monster appeared, silently. It was brown and white. It just stood and stared at us. I screamed and ran. The stingy nettles bit at my legs and the brambles clung to my clothes. In my panic I ran the wrong way and stopped at a dirty ditch at the edge of the field. What could I do? Jump the ditch and maybe land in the mud and be scolded for dirtying my summer dress or stay and be attacked by the brown and white monster? I squeezed myself deep into the bushes but the monster knew I was there.

Just then my friends appeared. "He won't hurt you. Look," one of them said. I watched as the group of children stroked the Lassie Collie dog. "Come here and let us show you." Two of the little boys took my hands in theirs and placed them deep into the long, soft, coat. I was smitten! I found this animal so amazingly warm, loving and gentle. I have no idea what happened but it was love at first touch! From that moment on I was hooked on dogs!

"Take that back where you found it," came my mother's voice from the house as I bought home yet another canine I had found!

"But it's lost. But it's a stray. But it's been ill-treated." I pleaded.

It took a year of pleading until mother finally gave in and we acquired a little bitch puppy called Bunty. She went everywhere with me. There was little traffic then and she didn't have a collar or lead. One night I went playing on the local school roof with my friends and Bunty must have strayed off with boredom and was run over. I lost my voice that night. I remember watching the car driver put her in a sack.

A year later I saved up my pocket money and bought Sue for two shillings and six pence. Sue was a little black and white Border Collie pup with floppy Spaniel ears.

I bought books on training dogs and taught her to 'heel' on and off the lead. I taught her to stay and many other tricks. Once in the park I made her sit and stay and I walked so far away that she couldn't hear me when I called her. There were many people in the park and a man asked me how I had trained her to do such a thing. He was quite amazed that Sue had sat and stayed for so long.

We had some wonderful times together. We went up on the hills whenever we could and we would be together with nature. I always felt I was with God when I was on the hills and surrounded by the beautiful green grass, the golden corn, the butterflies and little yellow cowslips. I loved to watch Sue sniffing in the rabbit holes and jumping up as a bird took flight. I would spend hours at weekends enjoying the peace and calm and just watching her play. Sue had to be put to sleep when she was 4 years old as she had developed fits and there was one she did not come out of. It was a dreadful day.

Later on I bred and showed many Whippets and Spaniels and we had two Jack Russell Terriers. We also had many other animals: pigs, sheep, ducks and geese and all sorts. Unfortunately my husband's family business went into liquidation and we had to part with just about everything. Our family, our animals, and our belongings all ended up living in a caravan.

We kept Dempsey as he could be rather bad tempered at times and of all our animals no-one would understand him. Dempsey passed to spirit in 2005 aged 18 years. A couple of days after his passing I had the most amazing experience. My younger daughter was in the computer room and as I opened the door the whole room seemed to be filled with the energy of Dempsey and it spilled out through the doorway. I was quite taken aback. We all sensed that we had 'seen' Dempsey on several occasions after his transition. The day he was put to sleep my husband was up the allotment (community garden plot) and he 'saw' Dempsey at exactly the time he was being put to sleep. I also 'felt' that was where Dempsey went.

As Dempsey had grown older I hadn't walked him much and once he was in spirit I walked even less. I was putting on weight and feeling rather 'shut in' and longing to walk in the countryside again. We all agreed it was time for another dog. We went to a rescue centre and met Patch. Patch is a Brindle Lurcher but he has a *white* patch on his chest. As Dempsey was small, Patch is huge! He is well behaved and appears not to have been ill-treated in his 18 months on this planet.

I have learned how to be the alpha male, or is it alpha female? I go through all openings before Patch. He remembers, I don't! He is always fed last too but he whines somewhat. This is reminiscent of his days in the rescue kennels, perhaps he was the last to be fed. We are training him to be quiet and he is improving.

A while back we had our first fall of snow this winter. I took Patch for a walk in the woods. There is a little lane to go down and then it opens out into the woods. As I turned the corner I beheld the most beautiful sight. Everywhere was covered in the purest, softest, whitest snow. No-one had stepped on it before me, not a single foot print. It was a magical sight and as Patch and I went on our walk I thanked God that I was able to discover the incredible love in monsters and black tails and walk with them in such beauty.

MEMORY'S GHOST

C. R. Nichols, California

*"Written 2-11-2006 on Fish Row in
Folsom State Prison, California"*

"I'm stuck in Folsom Prison, and time
keeps draggin' on . . ." -*Folsom Prison Blues,*
Johnny Cash. I used to get a kick out of
that song—never imagined I'd be experiencing it first
hand some day.

But here I am, and Johnny was right, time does keep
draggin' on. So, what went wrong? Well, nothing particularly sensational, not one of my antics, no matter how
hard I've tried to get attention, have ever shown up on
the evening news, local or national. I doubt that I have
ever even been mentioned in any prominent place in
the local news paper. Just a lot of relatively small things
all collected together to make a big thing.

I grew up angry. It seemed I always had to fight for
everything I wanted. I'll have to admit, I still feel anger
about a lot of things but I'm working on how to resolve
it.

Recently I've discovered that I seem to have a knack
for taking a few words and sort of weaving them together

in interesting ways. So, in my spare time (and I've got lots of it) I write a line or two of poetry, I discover amazing things about myself that way. Here's a poem I wrote back in February—it seems to be hinting that I may need to do a little forgiveness work along with the anger management. I call it *Memory's Ghost.* . .

Late night haunts the ones you've let down
the most.
Unspoken words, that look in the eye, of
memory's ghost.

No way to change what's already done.
There are some things in life we can't outrun.
Would it matter if they knew the pain I feel,
that rips at my soul and nothing can heal?

The look in the eye, the broken heart
shattered.
No cares, huh! Screw it all, that's all that
mattered.
"You only live once!" I said to all who would
listen
Now isolation's got my tongue, regrets that
scream, "Life I'm missin'!"

Echoes—then silence! Fear—then violence!
Laughing while crying! Living while dying!
Hoping while waiting! Loving while hating!

Late night haunts the ones you've let down
the most
Apologies, void here in memory's ghost.

Written 2-11-06 on Fish Row in Folsom State Prison,
California.

I used to spend a lot of time writing with spray paint on walls, signs and basically anything that didn't move or fight back. It was quite a rush to put my unique brand out there in bigger and better ways than the "competition" without getting caught. It never really occurred to me how wasteful and destructive it was. I only wanted to be noticed and appreciated, and was going about it in the only way I knew how at the time. Now I'm finding pen and paper much more satisfying and productive. Thanks for taking the time to hear me.

If you would like to drop me a line, I'm not expecting a change of address anytime in the near future, and I've got plenty of time to write you back. My contact information is listed in the back of the book.

Someday My Prince Will Come

Selidia Juniis-Johnson, New York

"It was time to make a choice. I could live
in fear, or I could live in faith . . ."

Once upon a time and they lived happily ever after: these are the bookends of fairy tales. I read these lines so often I accepted them as truth, looking for something external to bring happiness, peace, and satisfaction into my life. Yesterday is gone into memory, tomorrow is yet to dawn and today seems to pale against the days past.

"The whole world is a stage" it's been said. I now know that I have been unconsciously starring in the drama of my own life in many different roles: the child, the maiden, the young bride, the deserted wife, the other woman, the divorced woman, the maturing woman, the mature happy bride, the widow and now, happily a grand-mother.

As I mused, my poet's heart spoke as my hand penned these lines:

What Price Me?
Shall I measure in dollars,
Shall I measure in gold,
Shall I measure in success or
Shall I measure by the depth of my soul?

Life is worth living, but by whose equation?
My sorrow may be your elation.
When you check your positives against your
negatives
We find that everything is relative!

Who chooses my norms and my status quo?
Who will control my life's flow?
I know, but do they, that I want to BE
The question is, but where's the answer:
What Price Me?

By thought I am where I am. Some years back I awoke in the darkness of the night, just widowed and filled with fear. I heard a Voice speak to me, "What times thou art afraid, TRUST IN ME." Peace and calmness filled my soul. The new day finally dawned, being shut down and shut up is no longer for me.

It was time to make a choice. I could live in fear, or I could live in *faith*, for One with GOD is the majority.

I am a majority of ONE.
The many fractions of my MIND and BODY
stretch themselves toward the fulfillment of
acting in concert and harmony to achieve
the ultimate continuity
of BEING ME.

Today my soul is free in Christ. Joyfully, I add my own definition of freedom, that is to "inhale and exhale at leisure." I now allow SPIRIT to express in me, as me, and through me. I accept my divine right to live, laugh, love, forgive and be forgiven. I am alive, alert and aware. My consciousness daily expands. I transform any negative energy sent to me before I transmit that energy; thereby I transcend the experiences of my life's drama.

I let the "SON" shine in my heart. His Peace is within me, "as only the The Prince of Peace giveth." The peace which surpasses all understanding, not once upon a time, but for all time.

There is ONE Presence, Power, Love, Peace, Spirit, that is GOD, My Beloved I AM. I am one with My Beloved. The Bible verses I read in childhood become clear to me very suddenly. I see the LIGHT.

"In the beginning was the WORD.
And the WORD was with GOD,
And the WORD was GOD.
...And the WORD was made flesh
and dwelt among men."

The choice was mine. The choice, now, is yours. Will thou be made whole? Go in Peace or remain in pieces! I chose peace. Now, my heart proclaims—*my prince has come!*

MAGIC GLASSES

Alison Pothier, England

"To create a different reality takes the courage of a new set of eyes and a commitment to believe them."

M y grandfather once told me, "On the darkest of nights, you see the brightest stars. All you have to do is look up." In my darkest of nights, when the cry for help roared out of me with such strength that it shook the chimes in my room, I lay in a heap on the floor wondering if I'd ever see the stars again, why they were not shining down on me; maybe things were exactly as they seemed—as dark as the night.

If this was all there was, and all was as it seemed, in black and white without colour nor meaning or purpose to it, then I had no strength to carry on. All the years of belief in something more gave way to my scream, a cry for help and for hope. The chimes echoed my call and, in that very instant, the phone began to ring.

A voice inquired, "Hello?"

I whispered, "Hello?"

Silence.

It repeated, "Hello? ... Alison, is that you?"

I answered, "Yes," recognising my friend's voice.

Confused she pressed gently, "Alison, you called me, are you OK?"

I hesitated, "No ... I didn't call, but my phone rang, didn't you call me?"

She responded, "No, I didn't call, my phone rang here, I had to walk over to pick it up. Isn't that strange? Are you OK?"

In that moment the stars came out.

Was it possible that heaven really was watching over me? Did they answer my call, my guardian angels, my loved ones, my heaven, my God? Had they literally answered my call?

Moved by the irony of the moment, I embarked on a quest to know empirically whether all was really as it seemed, in black and white, meaningless coincidence and occasional irony, or whether there *was* a possibility that everything was indeed synchronous, blessed, colourful and meaningful. Is it possible that there is magic in each moment and that nothing is simply as it seems?

I believed that if I could embrace the faith I had inside, and a hope that life could have colour and possibility, I could embrace the magic. Only then, in my darkest hours, could I see the brightest stars.

That night I began what has become a four year study of my truth. At first a survival technique, I never imagined it to become a language course—'heavenspeak'; it is the language of heaven. It is a personalised language of symbols, sign-posts, meetings, greetings, songs, events, numbers, dreams, feelings, insights, health, wellbeing, and so on. It is a language through which each of us can connect with the spirituality that lies within and around us. Learn the language, and see the magic.

I began a fresh journal that night, this time observing my beliefs and experiences in two minds. In the first mindset, I wrote everything as it appeared to be on its surface, colourless. In the other, I captured life as it would look if every coincidence was less than coincidence, if there was no such thing as irony, if I looked a little closer at what was happening and saw it with a different set of eyes. I assigned a meaning to everything, and gave it a little bit more colour and possibility.

I called this process 'wearing magic glasses'—a mindset of faith and belief in God's presence and the power within me to experience it in my life. Through the lenses I could see and understand my growth and purpose in each moment. I could forgive, accept, embrace, heal, and laugh again.

With my magic glasses on, I could experience the possibility of a different 'reality'. I could flip the coin and see another side, a whole new picture and potential; two sides to every coin, two visions of everything: 'All is as it seems' or 'Nothing is as it seems'.

Whenever I was overcome by doubt and despair, I just put on my magic glasses and had another look. For me, the answer was as important as choosing life itself.

And so it began, my life through the lenses, a life of living for the brightest stars. I studied songs on the radio, number sequences, dreams, coincidental meetings and greetings, angels, healing, synchronicity and all that presented itself to me. I observed it, analysed it, lived it, breathed it, and wrote it down.

In my quest to discover a new truth, I learned to observe life. And in every moment observed, every dream translated, I learned that heaven speaks – right to us every moment of every day. I learned that every moment is boundless in possibility, that life is full of everyday miracles, and each path is full of blessed and spiritual adventures available to each one of us, if only we put on our magic glasses. I discovered my faith and myself again. I discovered a purpose in my every breath! Life became meaningful, beautiful, and exciting because I could experience heaven on earth in every moment—if I made the choice. After years of 'research' and journal upon journal of the parallel realities that I have written on my quest, I reached a few simple conclusions.

I decided that if at the end of my life, I learn that everything is really all as it seems: irony is irony and coincidence is coincidence, then I will still be at peace as I will have lived a magical life. I will have discovered that reality is as it is written, and heaven lies within us. I will have written a lovely story for myself and celebrated the magic in life anyway.

I am also certain that, should I find out in the end that indeed all really is more than it seems, but I had chosen not to believe it, I will be utterly disappointed to have missed the show, to have missed the magical connections in my journey here on earth.

The truth is, these years have renewed my faith in the magic of life. In my exploration, I have learned that to choose to walk through life in communion with my "self" and my spirituality, smiling at every small coincidence and following through when the sign-posts suggest a clever courageous turn, is to live life as it is meant to be for me: connected, supported, full of possibility and the ability to see in each moment a new meaning. With my glasses on, I am never alone. No pain is in vain, no loss without gain, no person without significance. Like light in a dark room, there is nothing to fear because life becomes a journey of faith. I feel excited that I can participate fully in every defining step—life with all of its trials and all its celebration.

However dark the night, I will always see the stars.

To create a different reality takes the courage of a new set of eyes and a commitment to believe them. May you always wear magic glasses to stand in awe of your life. Better yet, I wish you the blessing of perfected vision.

BEYOND SURVIVING

Matthew Ward, England

*"I was perceived as being Mr. Friendly and Helpful,
yet inside I was constantly criticizing myself."*

It is a strange thing this life we live you know! You are never really aware of what is coming and what obstacles you are going to have to overcome, only what has gone before. You remember hard times you have faced and the emotions you have felt. Still you press onwards without really knowing why and continuing on as you always have done. Well, I am here to tell you that survival and surviving is about more than just continuing and going on. It is about actually facing oneself head on and really knowing, loving and befriending the person inside no matter how hard or difficult it seems at the time.

Believe me, this isn't an easy thing to do and it has taken me years to accomplish. And if I had not accomplished this I would not have written this story you are about to read. My story is simple and yet one that is often so easily overlooked. It is basically about being comfortable with yourself when you are out or alone, learning to enjoy spending time with yourself. I can tell you I now thrive on this alone time and enjoy the prospect of it, knowing I can read a good book, listen to some nice music, meditate, or whatever else I feel like doing. Unfortunately my life hasn't always been like this and this is my story.

Ten years previous I was busy in two jobs, one in the morning making sandwiches and another in a coffee shop wiping tables. I was, one could say, lost. I hated alone time with a passion. When I was at home the TV was on constantly, I videoed programmes while I was at work and would watch them when I returned. My social life was non-existent. All I did was work and watch TV. I avoided living and facing life, as if someone had come along without telling me and removed a part of me. The thought of being with myself and spending time with myself doing nothing was far too scary.

I didn't know this then but the thought of facing life was too painful because of the traumas I had faced previously. One could actually say I was running away from living, but nobody knew. Everyone I worked with thought I was a perfectly happy and friendly man. Except the opposite was true, because I'd never really dealt with the trauma of my dad dying in a gas explosion when I was twelve and a half whilst we were on holiday in France. To lose your dad when you are prepared for it is a bit easier to take than just suddenly having him taken without warning.

Now you would think this would be enough to cope with but oh, no, not for me. Next I went to boarding school and faced the traumas of being a boarder with low self esteem *and* was coming to terms with losing a dad. The boys tried to be friendly but I wasn't able to cope with it and became misunderstood and alienated. This led to what can only be described as the worst four years of my life where I was emotionally bullied and constantly ridiculed. To top it all off my mum decides to have a lesbian relationship and I am left trying to understand why, when and how. So you can see now why it was easier to avoid life rather than face it.

However, avoiding facing life and just surviving did not do anything except make me miserable. It was almost as if a part of me needed to be filled. I was a shadow of who I could be and did not know how to be me let alone who I really was. Instead I perceived further study and gaining knowledge as a way forward. This enabled me to make friends and make changes but all I really did was to change working for studying. I was still avoiding living and merely surviving. I was perceived as being Mr. Friendly and Helpful, yet inside I was constantly criticizing myself.

Eventually though, things did change beyond recognition after reading a few self development books. Maybe it was the fact that I never lost hope that things would change and be better. I don't know. Anyway, I got a place at university after believing I never would and left the town I had lived in since the age of five. It was incredible and yet scary at the same time. Suddenly I couldn't hide behind work and study and didn't know what to do. So I replaced studying with over socialising. I was out nearly every night of the week at badminton, mountaineering, the movie club and clubbing. You would think from joining all these clubs I would have lots of friends. But I had about two and they were in badminton and that was it.

You see, none of it was real. Again I was surviving and replacing one busyness with another. The problem was that I didn't realize that's what I was doing. It is only in hindsight years later that I can see it. I was still avoiding facing me and who I was. A voice inside me was crying out for some acknowledgement. It is only now ten years later that I can actually face what I was avoiding. Now I can say that I am now living as opposed to surviving and in touch with who I am and what my needs are.

I can do this as I am now facing all the traumas that have gone before and not running away from them. Although I'm not working at present, I can say one thing: I am more connected with my feelings and myself than ever before. So what's the secret and how did I manage it? The answer is simple, to simply enjoy being you and not run away from who you are when with friends. What I mean by this is allow yourself to have your own interests different from your friends and some quality time on your own enjoying your own company.

When you are on your own allow yourself to enjoy simple pleasures such as seeing the steam rising from a hot drink or smelling freshly baked cakes/ bread in the oven. There is nothing better, I can tell you. For me it was as simple as getting a colouring book and enjoying colouring again with crayons, then taking up a creativity course for my art. Once I discovered my abilities in art and being creative I enrolled in a Foundation Art course. This enabled me to gain confidence and a belief in my abilities before I went on to university and did a three year degree course in art. This then resulted in my getting a 2nd degree qualification after discovering I could paint only four years earlier, quite an achievement, eh!!! I was absolutely thrilled and so glad to have taken the time to discover what I liked and to face myself head on and know what and who I actually was. When you take time to get to know yourself and face who you really are, it is amazing what you can achieve.

LETTER TO MY STEPDAUGHTER

Irene Humbach, New York

*"A Mother Bear type of protectiveness
rose to an almost fever pitch within
me, taking me by surprise."*

Last night we met your new boyfriend. At dinner, I watched your nervous face glancing first at Daddy, then at me, to see if you could pick up our impressions. Our opinions still mean so very much to you, although you try, at times, to act so independent and self assured. You looked shy, flushed and very young—hopeful, yet wary.

"So what do you think?" you asked, offhandedly, in the ladies room when we stepped away from the table.

"He seems very nice," I said, thinking silently, *also nervous, trying to impress.* I can forgive him his bravado, (he's only 18) and was secretly pleased with his politeness, intelligence, and sense of humor.

What I didn't tell you was that I felt a reservation in me; a sensing that he might be more words than actions —that you could get hurt. A Mother Bear type of protectiveness rose to an almost fever pitch within me, taking me by surprise.

"Be careful," Daddy said to me later when I shared this with him. "Give the boy a chance."

I was shocked at how much I wanted to get in his face and warn him not to mess with my girl—or he'd have <u>me</u> to contend with! Me, the girl, the woman who never thought she had it in her to be a Mom, ready to take this guy out in a flash if he stepped across the line and even *unconsciously* hurt or neglected you!

In our healing class, my teacher, Jason, talks about how things co-arise: a hammer looks for a nail, and a nail, a hammer; the existence of one calling forth, simultaneously, the existence of the other.

You, my stepdaughter, are calling forth a mothering in me, when I thought I had permanently grieved its' non-existence. I know now, it simply lay dormant in fertile, rather than fallow ground, waiting for your sunshine and your rain.

Gratefully,
"Mom"

INNER LISTENING MAKES THE DIFFERENCE

Kathryn Pape, West Virginia

*"With no one here to guide me, I prove again
that my answer is right here in me."*

The scene is late night in the Children's Ward of Cornell University Hospital. A young boy is lying in bed moaning, clasping his head with his two chubby hands. That boy is my son, David.

Sitting on his bed, I realize nothing as serious as this has ever happened to our family. But yesterday, everything changed! The unexpected vomiting, his walking into the wall and the crossing of his right eye caused me to call my physician. Years earlier, that physician had delivered David at home with all check-ups reading normal.

"An inward turned eye or lazy eye is not uncommon for children under the age of 5," she advised. "But vomiting and headaches mean something more serious. Get him to Jersey Shore emergency room and request an x-ray. I'll call ahead."

While driving to the hospital forty miles away, I began to hear a message, words from deep inside, **"CAT scan! David! Brain tumor!"** My heart began to ache as I raced up the road.

The message repeated, **"CAT scan...!"** Then as if knowing just what a mother needs, these heart-softening words followed, "He will be all right, this is his plan."

The word "plan" was right for me since I taught Personal Idea Development, a class on how to take an idea into a project and nurture it to completion. David, his siblings and many local children were learning this in my day-care.

Shortly after arriving at the hospital and assured that he would be all right, I requested a CAT scan. The staff disagreed but I refused to leave without a CAT scan, listening to my inner voice.

An hour or so later I was in a conference room facing numerous doctors seated in a semi-circle. The topic? *Why had I requested a CAT scan?*

I answered, "My inner listening, my intuition! You found something, right?" I saw the scanning results, which revealed a brain tumor. That is when I shared with them my parent's teaching me about "Special Intuition." According to my parents, I could recognize it by messages accompanied with warm inner feelings. These messages always keep us safe when listened to and followed.

David needed to get to Cornell University Hospital as quickly as possible. He was taken by ambulance to an awaiting staff. Meanwhile, I drove home and made arrangements for my children's care, packed some items for over night, and left with my husband, Jim, for New York.

We arrived in New York uncertain of the next steps. Jim went to fill out paperwork while I was escorted to

David's room. David squealed in delight seeing me again; the IV needle was still in his ankle.

The assigned doctor arrived having studied the scan results and scheduled a radiation treatment the next day around 3:00 p.m. He left saying "I think it is very small and caught in time."

Time passes and we are in David's new room. David is quiet and looking at the IV in his left hand. Lying there in a pale blue hospital robe, David asks, "Mommy, why does my head hurt off and on?"

David is only three so I ask him, "What does on and off mean, David?"

"It comes and goes, Mommy and it hurts. Oh, Mommy." Suddenly David grabs his head and begins to moan.

A thought shoots through my brain, **"contraction!"** Then I hear the words **"labor contraction."** Like lightening, the words **"time it,"** shout out of my soul. Scenes of David's birth and the timing of the contractions flash before me.

More messages! It would be easy to ignore the messages! How easy to distrust any voice from within. How much easier to request pain medication and put David to sleep. Yes, how much easier "not" to trust!

Through personal research I understand how thoughts strengthen or weaken a person. I decide to test the strengthening truthfulness of these messages. Working with energy I always use a muscle resistance test called Kinesiology. K-testing shows that reliable, (balanced- truthful) readings come from a hydrated, water satisfied, body. I am thirsty!

So before testing, I fill a glass with water several times and drink it all. Next, I make a positive statement in the present tense, "I am to time these contractions."

Being right handed, I bend and stiffen my right arm. Using two fingers from my left hand, I push down on my right wrist and suddenly release my wrist. My right arm springs up toward my right shoulder. A healthy bounce is there! A weak or missing bounce means not to follow the messages. The statement has not weakened me. The message to "time it" is true and right.

Now that I have my guide, I will trust and time the headaches. Like cause and effect I feel a rush of warmth fill my body and peace is there. I am making a difference for David and helping him with his plan.

"David," I say, "cry softly when it begins to hurt, and cry louder as it hurts. Keep crying until it goes away. Then Mommy will know what to do." David nods and gives me a weak smile. Another headache is starting. As David's moaning increases and then tapers, I recognize a wave pattern. I look for a clock or a stopwatch. There isn't any.

I start counting the seconds from the beginning of the contraction to its peak until it tapers. I count the seconds between onsets of the headaches, as part of the impression was "labor contraction." It is important to know how far apart they are! The next five minutes yield three more wave patterns.

I call the night nurse and tell her about timing the contractions and the behavior of the tumor. Her response is a gasp as she runs out of the room. This IS important!

I listen and believe in my inner voice! With no one here to guide me, I prove again that my answer is right here in me.

Whatever is to happen to David, I know that I am honest with myself and can live with my decisions concerning David. And the difference I am making for David is his life, his plan.

Apparently the tumor is growing. David faces radiation the next day. The nurse returns and explains: radiation creates heat and heat creates swelling. The swelling is causing David's severe headaches. David's tumor is already crowding his brain. More swelling will crush the brain tissues resulting in David dying.

She tells me the doctor *cancelled the radiation appointment and scheduled surgery early the next morning.* The nurse gives David medication that slows the tumor's activity and allows him to sleep.

Eventually, I share with the doctor the experience of listening and testing my inner voice. He smiles, glad there was no radiation session. The tumor he removes is the size of a "walnut" and is later pronounced "malignant."

Inner listening makes the difference. Listen, test, and trust your inner voice.

Postscript: Throughout David's treatment I continued to use kinesiology and inner listening. Three years later, at age six, he did pass on. I am currently writing a book about all that we experienced during that time.

THE POWER OF THANKS

Eva Gregory, California

*"Take the time to tell someone today how
much you honestly appreciate him or her."*

One of the best ways to practice positive, attractive thinking is through words of gratitude. Words are powerful things. From ancient times until today, scholars and wise people have believed words contain power.

The words we choose do have power, and they reflect a good deal of what is going on inside us. Whether you express thanks a hundred times a day, or haven't let these words pass through your lips in quite some time, the fact is the power of thanks can change your world today.

Thanks Changes Us.

When we have a heartfelt attitude of thankfulness, greed and all that goes with it go out the door. It's just not possible for greed, envy, bitterness, jealousy, and all those other nasties to live in a heart full of gratitude.

People often attempt to change and grow by shedding old, bad habits. While a focus on what you want to change is good, the fastest way to achieve that change is to replace negative thoughts and attitudes with positive. Ask yourself what you have to be thankful for today. Keep your focus in the now. Can you walk? Can you read? Can you change? Are you in control of your own destiny? These are but a few of the things for which we can all be grateful.

Thanks Changes Others.

Here's a fun experiment. Take the time to tell someone today how much you honestly appreciate him or her. Now this does not have to be some soap opera moment with hot, romantic glances and swelling violins —although you can do that if you like.

Simply take time to think about what the person you choose means to you. What impact do they have in your life? How do they make your world richer by simply being there for you? Once you have zeroed in on that, take a moment to tell them sincerely how you feel and thank them for their contribution. Now watch their eyes as you tell them.

Thanks Changes the World.

Once you take the time to sincerely thank that special person in your life, you will have changed the world for the better. Now that person will take those good feelings and probably pass them on to others.

Think of the impact you could have on the world if you simply took the time once a day to single out a special someone and show them sincere appreciation. What if that person caught the "Thanks virus" from you and passed it on to just one other. Now what would happen if only one person a day began to do this? To think … one simple attitude and one simple action: changing you, changing me, changing the world. When you develop an "attitude of gratitude," you crowd destructive emotions from your heart and mind, become happier and make others happier too. I call that a win-win-win.

Letting the feelings associated with gratitude surface is one of the best ways to pivot from any negative emotions. Think of the people who make you smile and the people who you are blessed to have in your life. Then, think about the work you thoroughly enjoy. Finally, think about how great it is that you are able to sit in comfort and read this book. Wow! I bet I made you smile. See, it wasn't difficult and it works rather quickly!

Since reflection can turn a mood around, why not share the wealth? Instead of just taking pleasure from what has made life better, why not give some back? Call up those friends who are always there for you and let them know how much you appreciate them. How about that teacher who inspired you to continue your education that helped you land the job of a lifetime, or your parents, children, or spouse who encourage, support, and motivate you? It is so easy to take the people who you always see for granted, simply because they are always there.

But what if they were not? Letting people know they play an important role in your life and they are valued is one of the most precious gifts that can be given. And it's free! It is funny how praise, gratitude, and appreciation work. When you take the time to be generous with others, you attract and therefore receive more.

RECONNECTION TO MY TRUE SELF

Jackie Christo, England

*"Lying on that hospital bed I became aware of
a light inside of me which was just a speck."*

I was lying on the hospital bed feeling absolutely worthless! My stomach had just been pumped due to an overdose of tablets. This was not because I desired to finish my life, but because I was recovering from (yet another) drinking binge which led, as usual, to me being physically and mentally unable to cope. I am writing this with hindsight after much soul searching, recovery and understanding of myself. At the time of my experience I was completely in the dark and unaware of the hidden processes.

I was married with a beautiful young daughter and upon sobering up once again the guilt was absolutely unbearable! The guilt was at the angry, awful, aggressive side of me that would emerge under the influence.

My behaviour upon sobering up was to follow a repetitive pattern. I would attempt to please all the people around me in order to feel better about myself.

My attempts at being dutiful wife, mother and daughter didn't last long. How could they? They weren't me.

Eventually the other awful, nagging, complaining, questioning, dissatisfied, angry, hurt side of me would begin to emerge, and because I couldn't connect or articulate it—out came the bottle. My dark side was shoved into denial and my false self was strengthened by the repeated behaviours around alcohol. Consequently, I lost my connection to myself. I was lost.

It had not always been like this. As a child I was highly sensitive and psychic, often experiencing spontaneous altered states of awareness. I now recognise that I was naturally deeply connected to myself and beyond. My childlike attempts to describe these experiences were with phrases such as "feeling bigger," "growing," describing myself as a "big pounding apple as big as the room." When at times these sensations overwhelmed me, I would call out to my mum, who knew how to comfort and reassure me that everything was all right.

I remember being in a dance class at the age of about eight where we asked to pretend to be paper hats blowing in the wind. I BECAME the paper hat blowing in the wind. Even though I was shy it was easy to lose myself in a room of other kids and become the paper hat. I also became the wind around the paper hat.

My feeling was always of being "more than" myself. I was "everything."

As a small child I loved music, writing, and dancing. I could draw you a diagram of an outfit I wanted to wear or how I would like my room to look! I periodically kept diaries of my thoughts and feelings. I knew my likes and dislikes.

What had happened to cause me to lose my connection? My paranormal experiences faded as I entered my late teens. I was brought up in a male dominated household in the middle of two brothers and parents who were extremely bonded. This provided for me as a small child a stable environment in which I felt extremely protected and loved. However, although there was much discussion in our household, it was never on the subject of feelings.

Somewhere along the way I had internalised the belief that being a decent human being did not involve anger, aggression and dissatisfaction, things I then perceived to be bad traits.

As I left childhood behind, the fact that I was unable to understand, articulate or express my feelings became increasingly difficult and painful to deal with. All I knew for certain was that I was FEELING and at times was extremely uncomfortable.

For me, the "feelings" were always there. Sometimes I felt like one big feeling and at the same time guilty for feeling! It was like I had a skin missing.

Somewhere in my mid-teens I discovered that alcohol could provide me with an immediate escape route from the feelings which threatened to overwhelm me.

Alcohol also provided me with a false sense of nirvana. But my attachment to the alcohol also stripped me bare of any self-esteem, self-respect and self-confidence I may have had. The drinking was actually just a symptom. The core problem was that I could not articulate nor understand what I was thinking or feeling. All I could do was experience the feeling, but couldn't understand or describe it.

The turning point happened while I was in the hospital. I was visited by a member of an organisation called Crisis Intervention and asked if I would accept some therapy. Therapy started 8 months later, but my inner process had begun. I was blessed to be placed with a therapist who was extremely sensitive and patient. He instinctively knew how and when to push my boundaries, knowing that any perceived critical comment would send me back into my false self. I grew to trust him and slowly allowed myself to grow up.

I began to take responsibility for my life, which could not happen overnight. I used various support systems and some suited me better than others. I found AA, a spiritual programme, and a wonderful organisation, where I gained much. But I couldn't utilise the 12 steps effectively until I had reconnected to my real self, and let go of the false self functioning purely to please others. However, my passion to be well kept me going back to AA and the seeds that were planted along the way kept me growing—everything helped.

I read many self help books which led me to believe that I could create the life I desired to live by, and gave me various techniques to help along the way. I rejected anything which did not resonate with me and began to trust my instincts. I became stronger and took risks. I began to accept the parts of me I had previously denied, thus becoming more whole. This involved facing my fears of rejection and judgement. Through connecting with my inner child I chose to protect her against rejection and critical judgments.

People around me were not used to me having opinions and this brought difficulty in all of my relationships. I was responding in ways that were unfamiliar to them. Sometimes the emotional fallout from this was enormous, but I had begun my journey.

These are the rules I choose to live by today:

I allow myself to make mistakes.

I allow myself to change my mind.

I allow myself to feel angry.

I allow myself to choose how I respond in
any situation.

I allow myself choices.

I allow myself freedom.

Most of all I allow myself a voice.

Today I work as a therapist utilising all that I have learnt. I have been guided to train in alternative therapies and will soon open my own Therapy City in London. My ethos is to help others tap in to their inner wisdom. I have always known that my first work had to be with myself. Lying on that hospital bed I became aware of a light inside of me which was just a speck. But I knew it was there. I also knew it would burn brightly for me in the future, and I knew that in a feeling. I knew my work in this life was to find my truth and my voice and that my gift would be in supporting others when I was ready. I knew my light would shine and I would spread my message. This knowing leaves me to get on with my life, in freedom. My power is within this moment. And my life—it is just beginning! My angels continue to guide me, but now I listen; I am ready.

.

AFFIRMATIONS AND POSITIVE THINKING
Margrit Buschi, New Zealand

*"I was feeling confident that I would
get there on time, I could relax."*

Affirmations and positive thinking have been part of my life for a long time. I never really realized or paid a second thought to whether I actually believed them. But one day I got proof and the realization that they work.

Last summer I started a night class teaching personal growth and self esteem. Every week I looked forward to teaching, but I also had a day job and often ended up with a very tight schedule in getting there on time. I used the bus for my day job, because the buses here are very reliable and have a good timetable, eliminating the need for expensive parking.

Anyway, one day I had to work about 15 minutes longer than planned, but this was enough for me to start worrying about my timing. I realized that I was starting to think the worst and was feeling anxious, because I thought I wouldn't make it to my evening class.

Walking towards the bus exchange, and becoming aware of the negative thoughts, I decided to give myself a break from those worries and come up with a positive statement for myself. "This class is important to me and to the people who attend it. A bus is waiting for me to bring me safely to my class with time to spare." I repeated this affirmation a few times as I waited at a red light. I just closed my eyes for a couple of seconds and visualized the bus waiting for me and getting me to my class with some time to spare. I was feeling confident that I would get there on time, I could relax. I thought to myself there was no way it could not happen. I just let it go and thought whatever happens is meant to be.

As I approached the bus exchange, there was chaos everywhere. Streets were blocked with car jams, buses and people. So I kept repeating my affirmation that there would be a bus waiting for me to take me safely to my class.

I arrived at my platform and there was my bus, waiting for me! I was the last person on board and the doors closed behind me. I talked to the bus driver and asked, "Why were you waiting almost ten minutes?"

He replied, "I received orders from the control room to wait."

A similar thing happened, when my son Jan and I went to my daughter's graduation in Hamilton, in the north island. We flew up there and my daughter's boyfriend, Brendan, picked us up from the airport. The plane was a few minutes late, and Brendan was a few minutes late too. So all in all, we were short on time. The graduation started at 9:00am and we had ten minutes to get there. That was fine, but then we had to find a place to park the car. Brendan kept saying, "There is no way we will ever find a car park." As soon as he said that, I replied: "We are positive, and there is a car park waiting for us right by the entrance." Brendan glanced sideways and said that it was impossible, because it was utter chaos and those parking spaces would be all full and taken. I said that he could just go there and have a look; he could still circle afterwards. I closed my eyes and visualized the free car park by the entrance and thanked God for the space he would keep for us and for guiding Brendan towards it. Brendan kept on saying that it was impossible to find any space for the car.

From the back of the car came the voice of my son saying, "Just drive past the entrance and see, you have nothing to lose."

As we drove towards the entrance there was a car park right in front by the door. We were just in time for the graduation and it was beautiful.

Brendan couldn't understand and thought we were crazy. My response was, "No, not crazy, just positive thinking and believing it!"

I thanked God and the universe for that impressive show-stopping event. My conclusion is that I can relax about things I have no control over and leave it up to the higher power to decide. Next time my bus is late, or I am stuck in a car jam, I know it is just the way it needs to be, and if I need help, just ask for what I need, even if it is just a carpark.

PEOPLE WHO MADE A DIFFERENCE

Roy Martin, England

*". . . an angel of wisdom and
guidance appeared in his life."*

It dawned on the man that there were five people who had made a real difference in his life. It is because of these people that he is where he is today, and like Hans Christian Andersen's "Ugly Duckling" story, these people saw through his 'dowdy feathers' and recognised the swan within him.

He was raised in a single parent family at a time when this was unusual. Sometimes in the early years his mother would work two jobs a day to ensure the family was financially stable, so he had to spend time with 'aunts' who would mind him before and after school. Occasionally he would be left by himself in the evenings while his mum was out at work and learnt that if he was a 'good boy' everything would be alright.

He grew up being wary and quite fearful of people, believing that if he kept them happy and made sure everything was okay then he would be safe. Because of this he did not have any close friends, but living by the coast, his greatest friendships were with the sea and nature. He relished the stormy days when he could experience the power of the waves as they crashed over the shore and watch seagulls as they hovered motionless, high above in the wind. For him this was freedom, away from a world which seemed strange and at times unfathomable. Not surprisingly, everyone thought him a dreamer and that he would need to buck his ideas up if he was to achieve anything in life. However, for the boy, it felt safer in his dream world where nobody could get at him. Yes, it was easier to hide away from the real world.

As a dyslexic, education was quite a challenge for the boy and he was consistently in the bottom group of his class. This reinforced his poor self image and belief that he was stupid and not good enough. In the sixties dyslexia was generally unknown and kids with it were just written off as low achievers. It was not until his forties that he was to be diagnosed with this mental condition but by then it had already set in motion a life of feeling inadequate and apprehensive of people - he just knew he was an ugly duckling.

In the boy's secondary school Brian was an art teacher who was fun, engaging and most of all had faith in his pupils. Brian had a mean throw with the board rubber - you did not mess with him! However, he had the respect of everyone. Brian encouraged the boy in every creative endeavour, challenging his thinking and assumed limitations. The classes where stimulating and for the boy, an immense relief from the academic grind. Brian provided an environment where there was no failure - only creation, learning and possibility. At last, he was receiving positive, rather than the normal negative recognition.

At the same school, Jack was the deputy head master and like Brian, a character not to be messed with. Jack taught maths and eventually became the boy's form teacher. Jack would spend time with the boy showing him that with persistence, he could indeed work out the complicated calculations. Jack saw through the teenager's facade of 'I can't do this because I'm stupid' and patiently encouraged him. Through his support the boy was one of a very few in his class to pass the national maths exam. From the experiences with these encouraging teachers the boy developed enough self-confidence to take and pass the entry examinations to be accepted into the Royal Air Force. Although the subsequent two years of RAF academic training was at times a struggle, he persevered and excelled in the practical aspects to successfully graduate with good grades. Maybe he was not so stupid after all.

He spent many years travelling the world with the military gaining many experiences but other people's judgements where never far from his mind.

Since his early years had taught him to 'stay average and stay small' he did not always push himself and would often become frustrated with work, which he saw as mundane and unchallenging. This would drive him to run his own businesses and get involved with work outside of the Air Force. However, after many years nothing ever seemed to satisfy. Life was never as joyful and fulfilling in comparison to the people he saw around him whom he felt had it all! It was many years later that he was to realise that the 'Shangri-La' he saw in others was just an illusion, a façade, and their lives were not as rosy as he had believed. These frustrations took their toll and after eight years, his marriage broke down. Coupled with his unchallenging job, life became a huge chore, draining his energy and slowly stealing his life away. He was still being a 'good boy' with a wonderful façade, hiding his true feelings and needs just to fit in. Like so many others, he was living a lie but too scared to do anything about it! He still felt like that ugly duckling.

It was during the height of his frustrations that a friend's grandmother, an angel of wisdom and guidance, appeared in his life. Mary just knew when you were hiding from yourself and always asked the right questions. The questions would take the man on a journey to his inner most world from where he gained a better understanding of life. Yes, Mary knew how to be there for people. She and her husband were both well into their sixties and the man would spend joyous hours listening to their stories and asking many questions. It was during one of his many visits that Mary's words would have a profound effect on him. When he expressed frustration at not feeling he fitted in Mary said, "There's nothing wrong with you, you just think differently to most other people." It was as if the light had come on, her words gave him permission to truly be himself.

Years later, two other people would make an impact on his thinking and life. Joe was a senior officer in command of the man's unit and unlike most other officers would spend time with his people and really get to know them - he cared and it showed. Joe seemed to understand the man's frustrations with his job and encouraged him to see the bigger picture of where he could be. For the first time in his career someone listened and understood. This gave the man hope and spurred him on to gain the education he would need to change his job. A few years later he would be blessed with another mentor who also listened and encouraged people. Like Joe, Dave was fun, a good leader and had earned people's respect. Dave had faith in the man and gave him projects which he ran along side his normal work. The opportunity brought out his creativity in many areas from business to leadership. It enabled the man to realise and acknowledge his natural abilities, many of which had been hidden for years beneath his lack of self worth and ugly duckling beliefs.

Over a period of 30 years, these people had come into the man's life and made a real difference either by what they said or what they did. They had had faith in the man and they saw through his façade and insecurities into his real potential. They did not judge! That man is now me and because of the positive influences of these people I have been able to personally grow and realise that I am no longer an 'Ugly Duckling'. Today I dedicate my life to help others see that they too are 'Swans', and honour those for what they did for me.

LIVE YOUR LIFE BY DESIGN

Dr. PaTrisha Anne, England

*"I explore the challenges that are set in my life
and then I ask when I need guidance."*

S ome years ago I was happily married with
a young family around me to enjoy. I was
living in a foreign country and enjoying the
adventure of being a young wife and a mum.

Proudly, I used to say to family and friends back
home in England during our weekly telephone calls,
"I'm so lucky. I have a husband who adores me, our
children, and our own home." Little did I know that the
ugly hand of unemployment would drop a blow. My idyl-
lic world was ruined by divorce, financial hardship and
finding myself alone in a foreign country with three children, all of whom were under the age of five. I decided
I had to get myself and my children home to England
and begin a new life. I knew it would be tough.

Once back in England, illness also struck. My doctor,
a General Practitioner, sent me to see a rheumatologist
specialist based on the symptoms I was displaying: an
aching body, extreme exhaustion, sensitivity to touch,

difficulty in moving around, and poor memory. The specialist consultant diagnosed Fibromyalgia, a degenerative disease of the muscles with no known cure. She told me I would end up in a wheelchair and that I would have to put up with the pain and take medication for the rest of my life; there was nothing they could do to help me become well and whole again.

The consultant said that I had quite literally worn myself out. For the last ten years or so of my life I'd been running around as if chased by a tiger in the jungle. Even though I was only in my early forties, my body was all used up. It also occurred to me that the possible onslaught of this disease had begun several years ago due to the shock of my husband and I falling out of love and deciding to get a divorce.

As I reflect back I am grateful that this debilitating disease had chosen to nestle inside of my body, because I was given another opportunity to do what I need to do on this plane. Actually life is quite good apart from the physical pain.

Yes, somehow I have survived, just as it says in the song lyrics, *I will survive,* but in essence I have done more than that. Let me explain.

The nightmare could have begun, but thankfully my enquiring mind lead me to the local library and I began to re-visit the concept of positive thinking and PMA, Positive Mental Attitude.

Since childhood I'd had a PMA outlook on life. My parents schooled me well, having to leave their native country of India and build a life as young newly weds with just a suitcase and a £5 note in the cold of the UK a few years after the second world war. My beautiful mother gave me the courage to 'be more with complete elegance,' and my father showed me how to 'do' more.

So I left the consultant's clinic full of hope, not dread. You see I had been given the opportunity to help others find a PMA and devise a life purpose plan. I knew my maker and the angels were giving me a chance!

Through necessity I began teaching PMA at home. It made sense to work from home rather than find child care for my young children and spend my hard earned cash paying a stranger to look after them.

The teachings grew over the years and finally in the late 1980's I was able to develop a school based on my teachings, LCSi - LifeCoach School international.

There is a very simple nursery poem my parents used to sing me that struck a chord in my heart and helped me develop my coaching model.

I keep six honest serving men they taught me all I knew

Their names are What and Why and When and How and Where and Who.

–Rudyard Kipling,
author of the Jungle Book stories.

The main self-coaching tool I use with my students and corporate clients is what I have developed and named the 6-Step Coaching Model. It allows the person, or the coach, to ask open quality questions that lead to clarity and actualisation of the goal.

Today after much learning I am able to pass my gift of 'motivation' on to others. To do that I have developed many tools and courses, one of which is a workshop aimed at individual adults to design their lifestyle; it's a spiritual concept I call Live Your Life By Design.

Daily, with the rising of the sun I affirm my purpose to live my life by design. Each day I review my needs and consider my commitments. Those commitments are part of my needs. And when the sun sets in what ever country I find myself, I take the time to reflect and to ponder the day, asking myself the six questions (what, why, when, how, where, who) that allow me to live *my* life by design.

This is the system I have created to teach my students and clients. You, too, can use it—it is my gift to you. Use it in any area of your life to find the true balance and answers to any of life's questions you may have. Always ask yourself open quality questions when searching for an answer. Use the framework below to determine exactly what you mean when you ask the question:

> WHAT: What do I really desire and need in my life?

> WHY: Why is the goal so important to me at this time of my life?

> WHO: Who else is involved in my goal?

> WHERE: Where do I need to get training or funding for my goal?

> WHEN: What's my time frame?

This short poem says it beautifully:
> *Yesterday is history*
> *Tomorrow is a mystery*
> *Today is the present*
> *That's why it is a gift*
> –Eleanor Roosevelt

> HOW: By asking and answering quality open questions the HOW happens, as if by magic.

If my words hold any pearls of wisdom for you, then I am happy about that. Remember,

"Knock and the door will be opened; everyone who asks receives..."

Matthew 7:7,8

I speak with my angels every day. I explore the challenges that are set in my life and then I ask when I need guidance. All I can share with you and say right now, for now is the power, is to apply your PMA, enjoy the privilege of having the opportunity to choose your life and to *Live Your Life by Design.*

A PATH OF SELF-DISCOVERY

Lilia Escamilla García, Mexico

*"In my mind and heart there was white light,
pure enough to illuminate all, to reveal all."*

In 1998 my life was very busy. I was married and mother of Fernando, a three-year-old baby boy. I also felt happy with a huge and exciting challenge in my job in training. Everything looked like life had smiled on me with plenty of success and health.

Suddenly, my husband, Luis, had several health problems. I just couldn't believe it. When Luis and I met ten years before he was a very healthy man, and able to handle lots of working hours at his job. Now it was like being in front of a stranger. We went to several doctors, and were given no hope for a cure.

I had always trusted in working hard to make things happen, but I felt helpless and depressed in this situation. I felt trapped at work, having no time to attend to my husband as he deserved, and not even time for my baby Fernando. Thank God I had wonderful support from my mother who took care of my home and family.

Still, I felt guilty because my job required long hours and a lot of travel, leaving so little time for home life.

One day at my job, I was speaking to two dear friends, Mayra and Sara Maria, about my husband's health problems. I always admired Sara Maria Esparza because she is a brilliant, extraordinary executive woman, professional and very dedicated to her job. Sara asked me about alternative medicine for my husband. "What?" I didn't know what she was talking about.

Having always been a skeptical person, I didn't believe in magic solutions or miracle cures. However, Sara with all her patience explained to me about energetic situations that affect health. Since my husband had been sick for so long surely his energy must be down, so he had to cure not only his body but also his life energy. Sara was taking a training called "Basics of Energetic Consciousness." She told me that training changed her life. She suggested I call her meditation teacher and consider the possibility of alternative medicine.

I don't believe in things by chance, so that conversation was a step toward my path of self-discovery. It was amazing I even made the call, considering that my early beliefs were against anything that looked like "magic." In my religion this was like making a big sin. It was hard to get an appointment with Sara's Reiki teacher, Lourdes Hinojosa, but I insisted. Now I realize that it was not only for Luis, but also for me because inside I was desperately screaming for help.

Lourdes, who is full of love for everyone, gave me the appointment the next Saturday. It felt like I was coming home. We prayed together. It was the very first time I heard about meditation and Buddhist thinking. She suggested Reiki to help Luis in healing. I was supposed to help by praying and giving positive energy to him. I didn't really understand but each week I noticed Luis becoming more peaceful. I wanted to have that for me too, but I told myself: *he is the sick one not you.* I was so wrong!

While talking to Lourdes one day about Luis's healing process she invited me to the next course of Energetic Consciousness. Although my old beliefs began to stir inside of me, I accepted.

At first I wasn't sure what I was doing there. Then a very important thing happened: I learned how to pray and ask for what I wanted. I wanted to open my consciousness, to see, hear, understand and feel. Suddenly, in a moment, the change began magically. In my mind and heart there was white light, pure enough to illuminate all, to reveal all. I felt full of the inner peace I was looking for. Everything was the way it should be. I understood who my teachers were in that moment. There couldn't be a better teacher for me than Luis. He taught me and walked with me in that spiritual awakening. That path was so new; his illness was the catalyst for my self-discovery and spiritual path.

I began to enjoy going to the training. I learned all is perfect so I could trust in God to handle my problems and worries and know I had his Light illuminating my path and my being.

After that training I followed with Reiki I & II trainings. I learned about Unconditional Pure Love and finally understood I could trust in the Universal Power to make things happen. I could feel the Divine presence of God and His love in very simple things: the health of my son, the healing process of Luis, my parents' presence in my life. I understood that angels and spiritual guides are all energy that is around us, and that God gives us His Infinite Love. We just have to ask them to be present to help. We need to visualize all we want in a positive way, loving all, leaving the negatives behind.

I want to thank you, Luis, for your Light and patience. Only with you in my life was I able to see my path very clearly. Since that day when I understood all this knowledge, I have changed dramatically. I am compassionate with people. I realize the gifts life gives me. I now understand people in the world, and that all of us are desperately looking for inner peace. Because of my teacher Luis, I had the experiences I needed to follow my path of self-discovery. Although our paths have ultimately gone different ways, I will never be able to express enough gratitude to him for the 10 years our marriage lasted.

In the end, my other greatest teacher is my son Fernando. He is a sensible boy who has given me big life lessons with the clear and direct expression of his ideas, thoughts and beliefs. Together we have built a strong family through spiritual growth. He practices Reiki and also meditation. We are harmonious together and look forward to learning new things. We know we have each other and also know that our extended family will always be a support to help us reach our goals and to meet all challenges.

LOVE AND LETTING GO

Antonia Gomez, California

"We decided to let you, our white dove, fly..."

L ove is wonderful and what you learn along the trails of life is beautiful. I lost my Mother on February 10, 2006 after she had been on dialysis for fifteen years. I give thanks to God that He permitted her to be with me for those extra fifteen years.

My mother, an example of strength, encouraged me all my life. The legacy she left me is beyond words. She left me with the desire to be a fighter in all ways and with the knowledge that I can achieve anything I want in life.

Seeing her on that dialysis machine was difficult, but she always fought back when she was sick. Despite going in and out of the hospital somehow she always had a cheery smile and a sparkle in her beautiful blue eyes. The personnel in the hospital felt very attached to her and they called her "Mamita".

Every time she would go into the hospital I would pray to God and my angels that everything would be OK and that they would heal her. Before February my prayers were always answered.

One time a doctor performed an endoscopy on her which perforated her intestine and that time we really thought she was not going to make it. However, an emergency operation allowed her to recover. I had prayed that if He permitted her to live that I wouldn't sue the doctor who performed the endoscopy. Incredibly she made it through and God allowed her to live with me for another wonderful seven years. I was grateful for yet another wonderful miracle in my life.

The last time that she entered the hospital my mother was getting tired of being in this world. She told me that she was tired and that she wanted to go to God. I didn't want to lose her; it was so hard for me to let her go. During her stay in Intensive Care I kept praying for another miracle. One day while I was in the cafeteria I heard the code blue announcement with her room number. What an experience and pain that was for my heart. I told God what was happening.

With my prayer I asked God and his Angels what had happened to the miracle and their answer to my heart was *"have we not always given you what you wanted?"* I thought over and over and realized it actually was true. The biggest miracle was for her to be with God. I know her heart was full of happiness at the moment she went with Him. Finally I was able to say her: *Mother I am letting you go to a place where you will be happier and at peace.*

A farewell poem that I wrote to her later:
> During all the years you were here on this
> earth, you always gave joy to our hearts. You
> taught us to love unconditionally.

When we were children you always gave us your love. You have left a big void in our hearts, but we know that we have an angel in the sky that will watch over us and protect us.

You always taught us to be independent and that we had to look toward our future.

Even when you suffered you didn't complain so we could be happy.

We decided to let you, our white dove, fly so that the Lord could take you into His arms and take away the suffering from your body and make your wish for peace come true.

Mother, thank you for your protection and love, which will always be in our hearts.

You Daughter,
Antonia

With all of this I have felt encouragement in my life. Last year I went on a trip to Sedona, Arizona, and I had the pleasure of meeting several people who prepared my heart for what was going to happen in 2006. I feel blessed because what I learned during that week has helped me to accept with peace everything that is going on in my life right now.

MORE PEARLS OF WISDOM?

Do you have a story to tell?

Here is Your Opportunity to Become a Published Author!

If you are like most people the chances are very good that you have some pearls of wisdom that you need to dislodge from within and share with others. There is a wonderful healing quality in people's stories both for the storyteller and the receiver.

If you are interested in contributing a story to a future *Pearls of Wisdom* book, contact us now to reserve your chapter in an upcoming edition.

All you need to do is write your story, something inspiring, uplifting or humorous for people to enjoy. Perhaps a story that led you to a healing of body, mind or spirit, or something that touched you deeply enough that it compels you to share it with others. If the situation or event touched you, it is sure to reach out to others. Keep your story between 600 and 1200 words, and in English.

For complete information go to:

www.HeartInspired.com/Pearls.htm

Or contact us today for more information:
Heart Inspired Presentations
P.O. Box 1081, Bonsall, CA 92003
Tel: 760-728-8783 Fax: 760-728-7390
E-mail: Pearls@HeartInspired.com

CONTRIBUTING AUTHORS:

BARBARA ANDRANOWSKI: Barbara is an award-winning artist, creating art known as Baya Design Pieces. She is also a Feng Shui practitioner and blends Louise L. Hay's philosophy with this practice. Her increased delight in Feng Shui inspired her to create the Feng Shui Pieces Collection and Feng Shui for Pets. Barbara is a graduate of Seton Hall University in New Jersey and a certified Heal Your Life workshop leader. She continues education in metaphysical/spiritual topics to expand her awareness and knowledge. Bayadesigns@att.net; www.bayadesigns.com.

DR. PATRISHA ANNE: Dr. PaTrisha has developed a dynamic spiritual holistic themed course. Her background of struggle, hardship and ill health all lend themselves to her ability to coach and teach individuals how to design their own dynamic lifestyle. Her unique style of personal performance coaching focuses on inner empowerment to build confidence. She can help you to build your success pattern with holistic tools, applied focus, self-design and instigating workable lifestyle strategies. You gain in health, well being, and work life balance. PaTrisha Anne and family live in England. LCSi - Coaching Leads To Success, www.lcsi.co.uk, www.patrishaanne.com, +44 (0) 1202 389998

SUSMITA BARUA: Susmita came from India to the US in 1985. Professionally she is trained as a geographer and urban-regional planner with M.Sc. and M.A. degrees. Her passion to understand the Nature of Reality and Self from a Universal Perspective led her to discover her own unique path in life. She is a Holistic Practitioner, Sacred Cyber Activist, Speaker and Visionary engaged in raising human consciousness both globally and locally. She is committed to empower the individual and transform the planet through her enlightened writings, transformational workshops and creative ideas in diverse fields. To see her current engagements visit her site at www.seek2know.net

TAMMY S. BLANKENSHIP: As a workshop facilitator and certified personal life coach, Tammy recently founded Creating Success Stories, a business offering tools, support, workshops and coaching for helping professionals. Tammy is committed to having a positive impact on the world one person, one deed, and one day at a time. Tammy lives in Ohio with her two sons, Gabriel and Michael, and is available to travel for workshops, group or individual coaching. You may contact Tammy for more information by email at tblankenship@creatingsuccessstories.com or by phone 330-831-0233

DAWN BRADLEY: Dawn is a Licensed NLP Practitioner, Professional Life Coach, and Heal Your Life, Achieve Your Dreams Workshop Leader. She has been a Registered Reflexologist with the British Reflexology Association since 1999 and is also a Usui Reiki Master and Teacher. Dawn has produced her own guided Visualisation CD, which incorporates the NLP skills gained at Paul McKenna Training. Dawn has collated her knowledge and experience to develop her own fun workshops and private consultations, tailored to each individuals' own needs. You can listen to Dawn's CD and find information about workshops and consultations at www.healyourlife.co.uk

MARGRIT BUSCHI: Owner of Heart & Soul Counselling, Margrit is a certified Heal your Life, Achieve your Dreams workshop leader. She is also part of JCR (Intercultural Exchange Programs) and lives in Christchurch, New Zealand. You can reach her by e-mail: Margrit@actrix.co.nz or by phone: 0064 3 981 97 94

BARBARA AVRIL BURGESS: Writer, poet, psychic, medium, and therapist, Barbara is trained in several of the new energy healing techniques as well as being a Reiki Master and counsellor. She is also a Heal Your Life, Achieve Your Dreams workshop leader. Visit her website at www.yourbeautifulmind.com for more information. Barbara lives in Nottinghamshire, England and can be reached by email at barbara@yourbeautifulmind.com. Barbara is a great lover of nature and animals, especially dogs. She is a great believer in people helping and empowering themselves and achieving their true potential through personal development.

JACKIE CHRISTO: Jackie's life until now has been a pathway towards preparation for Therapy City, opening June 2006 in London, UK. It is borne out of her experiences of rediscovering and healing the child within. She has been working for the past 15 years as a holistic therapist qualified in Reiki, Massage and Hypno/Psychotherapy, and has a Masters degree in Addictions Psychotherapy. She has had various recent experiences which have confirmed to her that the time is right to use her gifts to support others on their journey. You can email Jackie at jackiechristo@hotmail.com and request details about her website.

REV. LYNN COLLINS: Lynn teaches and practices healing as a Reiki Master, Heal Your Life teacher and Religious Science practitioner and minister. She lives in San Diego and holds classes and workshops there regularly. She also travels, speaking at different churches and giving healing workshops. Her Reiki classes are designed for the healthcare professional and the beginner. Her clients include people who are in good health, have chronic conditions, life threatening diagnoses and/or emotional and situational concerns. Teaching people how to use spiritual principles to enrich and deepen the experience of daily life is truly Lynn's passion. Contact her at giftoftheindigoangel@yahoo.com.

NORMAN COUCH: Dearly missed father of Dawn, Julie and Pauline and the dearly missed Granddad of Paris, Chernice, Jack, Kyle, Lily and Isobel. Contact: dawn@healyourlife.co.uk

VICTORIA DEPAUL: Intuitive knowledge since childhood has led Victoria to the fulfillment of her life's destiny, to be a teacher of Conscious Creation. Victoria devotes her energy to communicating her ideals through seminars and personal coaching on Psicanica, a philosophy of spiritual development and self-discovery. Victoria lives in the awareness that we all share a divine relationship with the universe: that we are the Creators of our own realities and life will manifest itself as we believe it will. For information on Psicanica products or to request a seminar in your area visit www.spiritual-training.com. Victoria can be contacted at Victoria@spiritual-training.com or Victoria-depaul@psicanica.com.

KAM K. DHANDA: As a qualified NLP Master Practitioner, Advanced "Heal Your Life, Achieve Your Dreams" Life-Changing Workshop Leader and Reiki Master, Kam strongly believes that we all are much more than we think we are…and that we all deserve to live the life that we desire. Her own life has become one of rediscovery and being a channel of God's love. Her mission in life is to contribute towards the harmony of life by empowering people through her everyday life and her business "Empowering-Life". Kam can be contacted via email: Kam@empowering-life.com or through her website: www.empowering-life.com.

GAIL DIMELOW: Gail is English and lives in Catalonia, Spain. She loves working with people and has done so throughout her professional life. Her own search for harmony and inner balance inspired her to become a Complementary Therapist and Heal Your Life Teacher. She lives near a heavenly beach which she loves sharing with others through the holistic holidays she organizes. Gail enjoys helping others deal with life's challenges in ways that work for them, teaching them to let go of what is holding them back, and live the best life they can. Contact her at (93) 791 3372 or visit her website www.innerlight-travels.com.

SANDRA JILL FILER: Sandra, originally from Flint, Michigan now resides in Houston, Texas. She is a Certified Heal Your Life, Achieve Your Dreams Workshop Leader and Future Director with Mary Kay. She is passionate about guiding others through transformational workshops, study groups, and circles. In addition to Heal Your Life, Achieve Your Dreams Workshops, she offers goddess glamours, fairy-themed facial & fun parties for little divas, and skin care classes. Sandra is an Empowerment Circle Guide with the Woman Within Organization and a joyful volunteer. Visit her website at www.marykay.com/sfiler or contact her at 713-201-2020.

BETHANY ELIZABETH FRASER: Bethany was born with a love and concern for the daily challenges people face. That love and concern sparked the desire for personal empowerment. Her biggest love is working with people who have experienced first-hand severe forms of abuse and teaching them the tools to heal. She has worked with many survivors one-on-one and in group settings, teaching them tools for daily practice. Bethany Elizabeth lives with her two children and husband of 25 years and continues to teach personal empowerment. She is presently working on her first book. Contact her at: bethanyelizabethfraser@yahoo.com.

LILIA ESCAMILLA GARCÍA: Born in Monterrey, Mexico, Lilia studied Communications and also has a master degree in Developing Organizations. In 1998 she began her spiritual pathway attending seminars like: Energetic Consciousness, Reiki, and NLP. Her business trainings include management, leadership, and mental maps. Now she is studying languages to prepare for her new international responsibility at her company. With her participation in this book she wants to thank her parents Arnulfo and Bertha for their lovable support and her son Fernando for being a wonderful blessing. E-mail: lilya.escamilla@hotmail.com. Phone (52 81) 81 100 49 007.

ROZANA GILMORE: An Intuitive Empath, Reiki Master and Feng Shui Consultant, Rozana is a practitioner, teacher and writer, blending holistic methodologies to help others deepen their awareness and create a life that promotes health, happiness and prosperity. Rozana considers her greatest blessings to be her beautiful children and family. Her inspiration is her Mother whose capacity for unconditional love is immeasurable. Rozana's business, In The Moment, is located in Southern Nevada where she works as a Well-Being Consultant. Email: itmwhispers@yahoo.com

ANTONIA GOMEZ: Born in Mexico, Antonia came to the United States at a very young age, growing up in the small town of San Miguel, New Mexico. She currently resides in Whittier, California. She is a true believer in all the miracles God and His angels have done in her life. God's Love and Uniqueness is beautiful to her heart. Antonia is an Angelspeake Facilitator, trained by authors Barbara Mark and Trudy Griswold. Contact her by email at angelbabyr@yahoo.com or on her cell phone at 323-447-9896

EVA GREGORY: Eva is a master coach, speaker and author of several books including *The Feel Good Guide to Prosperity*. She has instructed thousands in person, on the radio and in dozens of teleconference training seminars and programs on how to create a life by design using the Laws of Attraction. Eva is regularly featured on radio and in the media and is a recognized authority on the Laws of Attraction. Her new radio show, The Thrive Factor can be heard globally on Voice America Business Radio. To learn more, visit www.LeadingEdgeCoaching.com or email eva@coacheva.com.

ANNE HUMBACH: A happy 88 year- old retiree, Anne has lived for the past few years at The Fountains, a retirement community in the beautiful Hudson Valley, NY, where she designs and sells clay jewelry to benefit a scholarship fund for the young people who serve the residents. Woodcarving and short-story writing are two of her other interests. Anne received an award from the AARP for 17 years of volunteer service as Tour Chairperson for a local Chapter, organizing day trips, dinner theaters, museums, overnight trips, and multi-day tours. Every chance she gets, she still participates in many similar activities, now happily arranged by others! Contact her at 845-677-9910

IRENE HUMBACH: A lifetime seeker and practitioner of spiritual traditions and alternative healing approaches, Irene incorporates these into her practice, assisting individuals and couples to open blocks to their softer heart energy. Certified in Body-Centered Psychotherapy and Kabbalistic Healing, she and her husband are also certified as Exceptional Marriage Mentors, supporting committed couples in deepening their journey together. She offers time-limited group experiences for women at least 2 years in recovery from addictions, who want to deepen emotionally and spiritually. Kabbalistic Healing sessions are available in person or by phone. She practices in the Hudson Valley, NY. Contact her at 845-485-5933 or at ihum@optonline.net.

JAYANTHI: Originally from India, Jayanthi currently works as a computer analyst, residing in Utah with her husband, a researcher. Both of them practice Vipassana meditation. In her spare time, she teaches some simple healing and meditation techniques at an assisted care living center. She can be contacted via email: jayanthi1333@yahoo.com.

SELIDIA JUNIIS-JOHNSON: Second born daughter of Paul & Margaret Irving, Selidia is a widowed mother of two children, a grandmother, and is retired from the travel industry. She is now following her life's passions, pursuing spiritual studies and sharing Quantum Touch (giving positive spiritual energy) to any who request it. She is a published poet and a leader of Heal Your Life, Achieve Your Dreams Workshops. Selidia resides in Valley Cottage, New York. Contact her by email at sjuniisjohnson@hotmail.com.

ANGELIKI GAEL KOHILAKIS-DAVIS: Raised on a farm on Long Island, New York, Angeliki learned to attune herself with all the blessings from nature. She is a poet, writer, singer-songwriter, British Horse Society riding instructor and a biodynamic farmer. She works with Dr. Edward Bach's flower essences and is a Reiki master. As an intuitive healer, Angeliki works with people, pets and plants. She volunteers to teach classes in organics for The Nature Lyceum. She is completing her Master's Degree in Human Development with dual concentrations in holistic health and sustainable agriculture. Contact her via email: valleyoftheangels@yahoo.com and at www.thevalleyoftheangels.com.

CAREN M KOLERSKI: Caren's powerful presence makes a huge difference in people's lives! As owner of Heart Wings Healing, she inspires and teaches people to create lives of possibility, allowing that which is within to fully express! Caren is a certified Stress Management Consultant, Heal Your Life, Achieve Your Dreams Workshop Leader, and coming soon . . . Laughter Leader! She has created interactive Elders of Excellence and Caregiver seminars. In Buffalo, NY, she facilitates a women's networking from the heart group called Powerful You! Caren is available as a speaker, consultant, life coach, seminar/workshop leader. Call 716-983-7714 or visit her website: www.CoachCaren.com.

KARI-ANN REGINA LAMØY: Kari-Ann`s business is called Regnbuen (Rainbow) in Bodø, Norway. This is where she gives healing sessions and workshops. Kari-Ann is a certified Reiki Master, Chios® Master Teacher, and a Theta healing practicioner. She is also a certified Heal Your Life workshop leader. Her Life experience has provided her with insight, empathy and Love for herself, other people and Life. She is dedicated to emotional healing and Love of Self as healing tools for people in all parts of Life. Email: regnbuen2006@hotmail.com Website: http://www. freewebs.com/windsochange

CAROLINE MANNING: Combining the key skills gained from her Registered Nursing and International IT Consultancy careers with her passion for personal and professional development, Caroline emerged as a qualified Life Coach and Complementary Therapist. She is an EFT Trainer, NLP & Reiki Practitioner and a Heal Your Life Transformational Workshop Leader. Highly intuitive, Caroline utilises this range of skills in a unique, powerful and measurable way for her clients around the world. Caroline lives in Reading, Berkshire, UK with her husband Chris and two daughters Maisie and Megan. For more information please visit her website at www.purplegumdrop.com or e-mail caroline.manning@purplegumdrop.com

ROY MARTIN, MBE: Roy has worked in the field of psychology, personal awareness, and organisational change and development for many years. He is an inspirational speaker, facilitator, consultant and mentor who takes people straight to the heart of the matter, enabling them to realise their creative and undiscovered potential! Roy has worked with corporate and government organisations, smaller groups and individuals both in the UK and abroad, helping them to fully develop their true abilities in a safe, uplifting and fun environment. He lives in the West Midlands, England with his young family. Visit www.thejoyforlifecompany.co.uk or call Roy on +441212415624

VAL MCCRAE: Val has professional qualifications in teaching and counselling and more than 20 years experience helping people to reinvent and transform their lives. She is also a Heal Your Life workshop facilitator. Val is a member of the Australian Counselling Association and a Certified Level 1 Life Coach with her own practice in the Lower Blue Mountains. Here she combines her skills, experience and intuition to help others achieve what they want and deserve from life. Val's strengths in coaching are her commitment to her clients and her ability to connect with them on a deeply emotional level. Telephone: 0431 213 396. www.valmc-crae.com, valmccrae@hotmail.com

ANNIE MILLER: Life coach, trainer, businesswoman and pre-senter, Annie has a creative background as a chef and still carries passion for great food and wine. Annie is the mother of two children and is journeying as a carer for her terminally ill best friend. Her inspiration is most derived from seeing people of all ages reaching their potential and more, after encouragement to use their own values. Annie lives in Sydney, Australia and can be contacted by email at lightstream@optusnet.com.au or by mail at Lightstream Pty Ltd, PO Box 2107, Boronia Park NSW 2111, Australia.

TERESA MILLS: Teresa is a spiritual life coach specialising in using the principles of Louise Hay and Angelic guidance as the core of her life improvement plans. Blessed with an exceptional ability to connect with people at a deep level, she has used this talent to create a highly successful travel consultancy business. Teresa now uses her Angelic knowledge and personal connection skills to help people who wish to move their lives to ever higher levels of happiness and achievement. Her approach is grounded and practical, and helps clients to understand their own spiritual needs, linking them with tangible life action plans for 'whole life' success. Contact her at angelway@bigpond.net.au

KATRIN MUFF: Born in Switzerland, Katrin has lived and worked on four continents. She is dedicated to the development of human potential. Equipped with degrees in business and astrology, coach-ing experience, a creative mind and open heart, Katrin provides coaching and training for people and organizations in challenging situations. Together with fellow coach Denis Tchicaloff she offers an exclusive coaching program for people who have achieved success but continue to have a desire to realize their full potential. Contact information: www.yupango.ch, katrin@yupango.ch, phone: +41 (21) 6016969, Chandieu 4, 1006 Lausanne, Switzerland. Katrin works internationally and is regularly in North America.

C.R. NICHOLS: Like many of us, C. R. (Chris), has been on a quest to find himself for most of his 30 years on the planet. In his case however, most pathways traveled in this pursuit have brought him close to self-destruction. Like Dorothy in the Land of Oz, just when the "Emerald City" has come into view, the beautifully sweet and fragrant, but very deadly poppy fields have drawn him off the path and put him to sleep. And as with Dorothy, when in that "sleep" we lose the connection to our hearts, our wisdom, and our courage. But also as with Dorothy, Chris has a deep faith in a Higher Power, and that will be his awakening. Don't be surprised if you hear of snow gently falling on Folsom Prison. If you would like to write Chris you can send mail to: Chris Nichols, T-31420, C.S.P. Sacramento, B-2-128, P.O. Box 290066, Represa, CA 95671

KATHRYN PAPE: Owner of Pape Creative Education Services, Kathryn spent 30 years in education research on cognitive curriculums specializing in personal energy/idea development and Kinesiology. She conducts seminars and workshops on Human Energy Conservation related to self-esteem, creative thinking and personal power. She is a member of Zonta International, Toastmasters International, and A.A.U.W., organizations that promote personal and professional excellence. Kathryn is the author of *Always Like the First Time* and other writings used in her training courses. She is a mother of 7, grandmother of 2 and resides in Parkersburg, West Virginia with husband James, her college sweetheart. Contact her at: pape74@verizon.net

NORMA GEORGINA RODRÍGUEZ PAZ: As one of only seven Certified Heal Your Life, AchieveYour Dreams workshops leaders in Mexico, Georgina also holds a Personal Development Diploma from Iberoameriana University, and is currently completing her Master's there. Some of the self-development courses she has participated in are: Silva Mind Control, Dale Carnegie Trainings and Franklin Covey Courses. With an MBA from Nuevo Leon University in Mexico, she has beena teacher in that school and in Monterrey University. She gives HYL Trainings in North of Mexico. She lives with her family in Monterrey, NL, Mexico. Contact her by phone at (52 81) 81-10-63-46-49 and by e-mail: norma_georgina@yahoo.com.mx.

DENISE N. PEREZ: With a strong desire to help others live inspired, joyous and rewarding lives, Denise founded PROPEL Coaching & Training (www.PROPELCoaching.com) and serves as a certified life coach and transformational workshop facilitator. Denise received her B.A. in Sociology from Princeton University, and will graduate from NYU in August 2006 with her second professional coaching certification. As an accomplished coaching and business management professional, she is currently taking a lead role in designing and implementing the Executive Coaching Program at the Support Center for Nonprofit Management in NYC. She may be contacted via email at denise@PROPELCoaching.com

ALISON POTHIER: Alison runs a centre for healing and development called Presence and Presents, in London, England. An investment banker by trade, Alison is also an intuitive healer, counsellor, and life coach. Alison believes that true healing is a process, not an event. She defines it as the return to the essence of one's true spiritual self. Alison calls this 'working from the inside out': exploring the inner beliefs that shape our outer reality. In her pearl of wisdom, Alison shares with us a tool that re-shaped her personal reality into a more magical existence.info@presenceandpresents. com, www.presenceandpresents.com +44 (0)208 332 6566

EVA-MARIA RIEGLER: Born in Austria, Eva-Maria now resides with her daughter in London. She is a sociologist, artist, and Heal Your Life workshop teacher. She can be contacted by email at evariegler@talk21.com.

DIANA RITCHIE: Diana's incredible story of self-healing and her transformation has touched thousands. Her struggle to overcome the debilitating disease of Multiple Sclerosis is truly inspirational. Diana has since dedicated herself to assisting others in developing and using their inner healing powers to overcome their life's challenges. Diana's transformation is a moving story that she knows will encourage everyone who is experiencing an illness or challenge in their lives to experience their own healing transformation and as she likes to say, it's time to begin "Healing the Whole Self." http://DRHealing.home.att.net and DRHealing@att.net

BECKY ROTHSTEIN: Becky teaches The Power of the Mind and Positive Thinking to improve the quality of Life. She lives in Israel and gives seminars, workshops and lectures in Hebrew, Spanish, and English all over the country and overseas. Becky worked for many years with different healing methods like Kinesiology, Reiki, and ways of relaxation. Since 1999 she has given lectures to whoever wants to change their attitude about Life, including parents, youngsters, doctors, nurses, social workers, teachers and psychologists. She coaches and provides private lessons. Becky can be reached at 972 3 6950 789 or by email to rbecky@ netvision.net.il

LISA K. STORY: Lisa enjoys living her dreams in the sunny paradise of Shell Beach, California with her husband, Doug and their beautiful children Sydney and Sam. She has spent the past 17 years working in health care and health education with a special fondness for women's health. Lisa became a Certified Heal Your Life Teacher almost nine years ago. Her mission is to motivate, inspire and support others in living a conscious life filled with the joy, health and peace they desire. She may be reached at lisastory@charter.net.

PETER TEUSCHER: Peter is a writer and a coach who emphasizes the necessity for each of us to develop a personal philosophy on life in order to increase our self awareness and in turn be happier individuals. After a spiritual awakening, he chose to apply a philosophical approach to personal and business development. With a keen desire to help others and to lead by example, Peter has written his first book which puts his life and personal experiences on display in an attempt to illustrate how the development of a philosophy can provide the foundation for all of life's abundance. Contact him at: peter@peterteuscher.com or visit his website, www.peterteuscher.com

MATTHEW WARD: While working in a coffee shop as a catering assistant ten years ago, Matthew began discovering his role in life, what he had to offer, and searching for the person he really is. It was as though he began to see the outside world for the first time. During this searching he attended a number of self-development workshops and discovered his true gifts of creativity, wisdom and sensitivity. He is now working on his autobiography and planning to train as an art therapist, having succeeded in achieving a degree in visual arts last year. Contact him by email at fubb212@yahoo.com

ABOUT PATRICIA CRANE, PH.D. :

Patricia is an author, speaker, and workshop leader. Her first book, *Ordering From the Cosmic Kitchen: The Essential Guide to Powerful, Nourishing Affirmations,* has received enthusiastic reviews. She discovered the life-affirming principles shared in that book through her own personal search for meaning and purpose. A meditation practice for many years has been the foundation for her growth.

With a strong desire to help others, she initially pursued an educational route, earning a Ph.D. in social psychology with a specialty focus on wellness programs at the worksite (primarily stress management). For several years she taught stress management courses at the university level and gave corporate workshops. But her heart was yearning to share something deeper. Having attended numerous workshops with some of the premier spiritual leaders of our time and studied personal development and spiritual books, she began to offer workshops in meditation, the mind/body connection, prosperity, Reiki Natural Healing, creative visualization, effective affirmations, breathwork, and more. Her work with Louise Hay resulted in leading international workshops and creating a powerful training program for personal growth workshop leaders.

In 1995 she met life partner Rick Nichols, and they began traveling and teaching together, plus collaborating on personal growth products. They now live in a beautiful country setting in north San Diego County on a seven acre ranch, complete with an avocado grove. The serene view across the valley nurtures and rejuvenates them on a daily basis.

Patricia's intention is to continue sharing a message of personal empowerment in co-creation with Spirit. She is committed to the expansion of the heart for personal and planetary healing.

ABOUT RICK NICHOLS:

Rick Nichols, a principal partner of Heart Inspired Presentations and an expert on human potential, is an author, storyteller and international speaker. With his inspirational, warm, and humorous style Rick has captivated audiences around the world. He is a speaker of many facets, at once a storyteller, poet, and philosopher, as well as a teacher and student of life.

Raised by a pair of alcoholic combatants in a domestic war zone along with five siblings, Rick learned much about coping with adversity early in life. Upon awakening the morning of his 17th birthday he had to face the fact that while others of his age were about to graduate high school, he was failing the 9th grade. It was on that day that Rick leaped from one war zone to another, as he joined the US Navy and went to Vietnam; there his education really began. He learned important things that the public school systems didn't teach: self-esteem, teamwork, cooperation, and compassion. One of the most important things he learned was that he is capable of learning, and that he has value; nobody had ever told him that before.

On a life mission to "Inspire people the world over to a higher level of thinking about who they are, what they've got, and how to bring themselves more fully into the world," Rick presents programs designed to shift a person's perspective, which opens them to a deeper self-awareness and greater potential for a fulfilling life. The rich diversity of Rick's salt and pepper background is sprinkled throughout his presentations. He has experienced the highs and lows of life, learned how to make the best of it all, and is willing to intimately share it with his audiences.

Patricia and Rick offer a variety of powerful programs and products for personal growth. For a current schedule and to see all their products, please visit their main web site, www.heartinspired.com. They are available to travel to your group for presentations. Their workshops, keynotes, and seminars include:

Creating Wealth From the Inside Out

Wisdom of the Ages from the Land of Oz and Beyond

Heal Your Life, Achieve Your Dreams Workshop Leader Training

Stress Management

Healing Breathwork

Success Strategies for Women on the Go

The Magic of Believing in Yourself

Contact them at (800) 969-4584 or (760) 728-8783 or write to P.O. Box 1081, Bonsall, CA 92003.
E-mail patricia@heartinspired.com
or rick@heartinspiredcom.

The following web sites will give you complete information on all of the programs we are currently offering. Be sure to take advantage of the many free online training opportunities you will find. You may also want to subscribe to our free weekly inspirational Internet magazine, Monday Morning HeartBeats. It is the perfect way to get your week started on a positive note. Free QuickTips for more successful living are provided every Friday to get you ready for the weekend. We are sure you will enjoy the free inspirational flash movie presentations.

www.HeartInspired.com

Our flag ship web site and the hub for all the sites listed below. From here you can learn all about us and what we offer that will be of value to you.

www.ChangeInsideOut.com

Take our online courses in meditation, creating wealth, affirmations, conscious weight loss, and more... all for one easy, affordable lifetime membership fee.

www.TakingABreather.com

Relax and enjoy the peace and beauty of nature, music and art. This four minute experience will instantly put peace and tranquility into your life, no matter how hectic it has been. Learn simple techniques for managing stress.

www.MessagesFromTheAngels.com

Angels are the part of God that appear to us on earth in a way we can understand. The angels constantly tell of joy, peace and love, for that is the only story they have to tell.

Take a moment for communion with the angels. They will inspire you with a renewed faith that all is well.

www.OrderingFromtheCosmicKitchen.com

Learn how to create and use powerful affirmations to improve your life in every way. Be sure and sign up here for Patricia's powerful e-course on affirmations and preview a chapter of her book, *Ordering from the*

Cosmic Kitchen: The Essential Guide to Powerful, Nourishing Affirmations.

www.HYLTeachers.com

A directory of trained Heal Your Life, Achieve Your Dreams teachers worldwide. Learn how you too can be certified to lead Heal Your Life, Achieve Your Dreams workshops.

www.ScienceOfGettingRichNow.com

Learn the mental and spiritual principles for becoming rich. We are always in choice, the Universe provides an abundance of opportunities and then leaves it entirely up to each individual whether to accept or reject them.

www.SuccessForBiz.com

Success Strategies for Life and Business.

Business topics include empowerment, self-esteem, creativity, stress management, workplace wellness, communication skills and presentation skills.

Personal growth topics include releasing old beliefs, increasing prosperity, finding your ideal life work, and more.

Other Books from Heart Inspired Presentations:

Ordering from the Cosmic Kitchen:
The Essential Guide to Powerful Nourishing Affirmations

by Patricia Crane, Ph.D.

The Essential Guide to Powerful, Nourishing Affirmations

Patricia J. Crane, Ph.D.

All 5 star reviews on Amazon.com!

Learn how to create and use powerful affirmations to improve your life in every way.

One hundred sixty pages in twelve chapters filled with success stories from cosmic orders and instructions on how to order up the things you want, need and deserve from life. Order your copy today!

"If you're ready to lovingly nurture yourself with positive affirmations, here's the book for you."

-Mark Victor Hansen
Co-creator, #1 New York Times best-selling series
Chicken Soup for the Soul

In the Flow of Life:
How to Create and Build Beautiful Indoor Water Fountains

by Rick Nichols

In The Flow of Life
HOW TO Create and Build
The Shell
The Falls
The Bubbler
Beautiful Indoor Water Fountains
For less than $25.00 in materials!
by Rick Nichols

Learn how to create and build your own beautiful and soothing water fountains for as little as $25.00 in materials!

"This is a most practical guide to making your own wondrous creation: your own personalized water feature. Enjoy!"

-Terah Kathryn Collins
Author of The Western Guide to Feng Shui